MEMOIR OF A
HOCKEY
NOBODY

They said I couldn't make the NHL,
so I went out and proved them right!

JERRY "TEABAG" HACK

Tellwell Talent
www.tellwell.ca

ISBN
978-0-2288-2802-0 (Paperback)
978-0-2288-2803-7 (eBook)

TABLE OF CONTENTS

Foreword...vii

Chapter 1   Marlene and the Canadiens (pronounced
             KANAdyenz)... 1
Chapter 2   The Move 7
Chapter 3   And the Band Played On 21
Chapter 4   Get Some Skates Kid 25
Chapter 5   A Different World...................................... 29
Chapter 6   The Mask... 31
Chapter 7   I'm on a Real Team.................................... 36
Chapter 8   A Rookie No More 44
Chapter 9   The Merger 52
Chapter 10   Valhalla 59
Chapter 11   The Golden Years....................................... 66
Chapter 12   Game Changer 69
Chapter 13   Destiny... 88
Chapter 14   Trial by Fire... 94
Chapter 15   Neckties, Contracts, High Voltage........... 105
Chapter 16   Business Time.. 108
Chapter 17   A Season in Hell..118
Chapter 18   Heeeeeeres... Johnny! 141
Chapter 19   Reversal of Fortune................................... 154
Chapter 20   Domination...161
Chapter 21   California Dreamin' 166
Chapter 22   New Horizons 174
Chapter 23   The Good, The Bad, and The End 196

Epilogue 215

For Brooklynn: Daddy loves his little
girl more than chocolate.

For Kathleen: My beautiful wife. I
love you with all my heart.

For my sister Marlene: Who passed away from cancer in
2005. You inspired my love for the game. You are still my
hero. We all miss you and we will see each other again.

For my friend Suzanne: Who is fighting the mother of
all battles, and doing it with a positive attitude, and a
steely resolve that is an inspiration to all who know her.

For Terry: My best friend for the past 25
years. Thanks for being my rock.

I love you Bro.

Foreword

I haven't written so much as a paragraph since high school English class over 40 years ago. So, you can assume that I am no Dashiell Hammett, or even Kirk Hammett for that matter. After posting some stories about my senior hockey days on Facebook, some of my friends responded to them by saying that I should write a book. And so, I did. I must say that it has been cathartic in many ways. Such a flood of memories came into my brain all at once. Trying to type them into a computer was a lot like pouring a really thick liquid into a funnel. It… goes… sooooo… slooooooowwwww. It seemed slower than molasses going uphill. I have decent typing skills, I can type about 90 words per minute, but half of that is backspace. Figuring that this was a "one shot" deal, I gave writing this book my best effort, and I hope you find my story at least a little bit entertaining.

I must warn you though… The hockey world of that time is a male dominated, macho-world. If you are a politically correct person who is easily offended, I strongly urge you NOT to read this memoir. I mean to say, buy the book, (we need the money), but do not read it. I'm sure it would make an excellent coaster.

Within these pages I use a homophobic slur. I now understand how hurtful, divisive, and harmful this word is. If this memoir was a novel, I wouldn't have used this word in a million years. However, I wish to portray a true story, and I did use that word, and many words like it, during my younger days and the time these stories take place. I wish to apologize to all my gay friends and family for using this word and others. I am sorry, and I am ashamed.

The tale you're going to read is 100% true. I'm sure that I have many of the details wrong, but I am writing about thirty-year old memories. I tried to limit the profanity wherever possible, but people said the things they said and I want to keep this story true as to how it happened.

Thank you to Dan Burnett for the legal advice. He assures me that if anyone sues me for what is within these pages, they will not win, (in his totally objective unbiased and expert opinion).

I found that I tend to write the same way that I speak, so if the text is a little bumpy, the fault lies with me. So, with that, I wish to thank my editors:

Brittany Ashwell and Stephen Greaux

Great job, both of you. You have my undying gratitude.

(But if this book tanks, I am completely throwing you under the bus. "It wasn't my fault, the editor's screwed the whole thing up!")

For everyone that asked me "Am I in the book?" You all get my standard answer which is: "Yes, but you die in the end."

I wish to thank Darren Lucier, Art Birss and Kevin Silzer, who helped me with what little research I did. Thanks guys, I will buy you a beer the next time we meet. Now, without further ado, and zero fanfare, here is my tale.

CHAPTER 1

Marlene and the Canadiens (pronounced KANAdyenz)

To quote Steve Martin, "I was born a poor black child… " (*The Jerk, 1979*). Okay I wasn't, but I certainly was a black sheep. I fully believe that I was born to be a goalie. It all started with my birth in the winter of 1961 at Burnaby General Hospital in Burnaby, British Columbia, (a suburb of Vancouver). I was the fourth of five children, (the rest are girls), born to Edward and Genevieve Hack. My upbringing was rather unremarkable. Dad drove a dump truck and Mom was a waitress. I was described by my older sisters as a "sickeningly happy child." I went to school in Burnaby where I lived the majority of my life. When I started working, that's when I moved all over the lower mainland. I have probably lived in every suburb of Vancouver there is. Burnaby is where world famous actor Michael J. Fox is from. I once dated a girl who had dated him while they were in high school. I firmly believe this alone makes me famous. I mean, c'mon, get out of town.

Our family was tight knit. My sisters: Marlene, born in 1955, Marjorie, 1958, Patricia, 1960, then Bonnie born in 1971. Bonnie being born almost 10 years after me, was supposed to be a boy. I had wanted a little brother very badly, but it wasn't meant to be. I always bugged her that she was an "accident". That was until my Mom heard me say that to her and Mom said, "she wasn't an accident, YOU were an accident." While growing up, us kids played together a lot, and fought like crazy. But still, the house was mostly a happy one. I have to say that my sisters were overall, very good to me. Other than pinning me down and tickling me, and occasionally putting nail polish on my fingernails, they were a lot of fun to grow up with. Trish went through a period where we thought the only words she knew were "shut up." We always had a roof over our heads, a car, (sometimes two), food to eat, and beds to sleep in. We walked a mile to school together, and usually came home separately. We were just your normal everyday family. I would put us in the "upper poor" class. Like I said, rather unremarkable.

My real love of hockey began during the Stanley Cup Finals in 1971 when I was nine. The Montreal Canadiens were playing the Chicago Blackhawks. My sister Marlene, who was following it, was rooting for the Canadiens, (because they were from Canada). It never dawned on me that 95% of the players were Canadian.

Since it was Canada vs. The United States: I was rooting for the Canadiens. I thought Marlene was the smartest person alive, and was my hero because of that. My memory of this time is very hazy, so I don't remember if we watched from the beginning of the playoffs or not. I vaguely remember the Canadiens knocking out the powerful Boston Bruins, but I mostly just remember the finals vs. the Chicago Blackhawks. Most of all I remember, Frank and Peter Mahovolich, Bobby and Dennis Hull, Chico Maki, Stan Mikita, Eric Nesterenko, Yvan Cournoyer, Jacques Laperriere, Guy Lapointe and Jacques Lemaire. This is when my passion for goaltending began. Watching Ken Dryden and Tony Esposito battle for seven games got me more excited than anything I had known before. I liked how Ken Dryden leaned on his stick during stoppages, and how Tony Esposito seemed to go to his knees every time there was a shot against him. I got so excited when Frank, "The Big M" Mahovolich, had a penalty shot. I remember he took a slapshot, and Esposito stopped it easily. Excitement overload. These were the greatest of days.

Growing up in my family, I didn't know that we had limited means. I mean, we always drove an older car which my Dad, who could fix almost anything, was always fixing. We always had second hand furniture. We didn't have the biggest house, and always had to share bedrooms. Trish and I shared a room for a few years and one night she asked me if I had started my periods yet. I didn't know what she was talking about, then she said "you know, Kotex!" I knew what they were for and I just told her no, I hadn't. I couldn't sleep that night because I was scared that I was going to start bleeding from my nether regions. I knew that blood would not come from Mr. Happy. I was thinking that some mysterious hole was going to open up and start hemorrhaging. My Mom explained to both of us the next day that only girls got periods. She didn't want Trish going to school and asking all the boys if they had started their periods yet. We also wore a lot of hand-me-downs and, if you were to ask me if I had to wear my sister's clothes, the answer is: not often. Both my parents came from large families (Mom had seven siblings, Dad had five) so we had a thousand cousins, and every so often we would get a bag full of clothing from one of my Aunts. She would give us the clothes from my male cousins that they had outgrown. Somehow, I just sensed that we couldn't afford for me to play organized ice hockey, so I never asked. Road hockey however, was a different story entirely. I went to Douglas Road Elementary School, (which surprisingly is still standing), and very early on made friends with another boy named, Mark Ferguson. He lived on Manor Street, which was about half way between home and the school for me. It is here that my real hockey story begins.

Mark Ferguson was friends with two brothers named Eric and Ian Frison, (pronounced FREEzin), who lived on Dominion Street one block up from Manor Street. There were a bunch of kids in the neighbourhood who would all congregate at Eric and Ian's house. They had the best driveway for road hockey. It was long, and ran beside their house and ended at the garage, which acted as a backstop, (which was very important). There were no windows on that side of the house, which was also important. We of course played with a tennis ball. Every once in a while, we would try to play with the dreaded, orange "hockey ball", but we always went back to the tennis ball. The pain factor was greatly reduced playing with the tennis ball. Everybody preferred that, except for the kids that liked to inflict pain. Luckily there weren't many of those, and they got outvoted.

The equipment we used was primitive to say the least. I remember making a goalie stick out of scrap pieces of wood from my Dad's workshop. The goalie pads were two pieces of foam from an old couch cushion, strapped to your legs with elastic straps. We had a regular hockey glove for a blocker, and then a baseball glove for the catching hand. We never wore masks, and for chest protection we would wear winter jackets under our hockey jerseys. Most of the sticks we used had the plastic blades attached to a wooden shaft. These things were the greatest invention as far as we were concerned. If your wooden stick blade broke, your parents could buy a plastic blade for a fraction of the cost of a new stick. Ice hockey parents didn't have this option. Also, as the plastic blade wore down, you could curve it like crazy. Everyone wanted to copy Bobby Hull in this manner.

If you used it long enough, the blade would wear down so that it was only a couple of inches tall, and the end of the blade would come to a point. It looked really cool and every shot you took would go up and hopefully "top shelf". All the kids loved "top shelf".

Danny MacIntosh lived next door to the Frison's, and his house had a huge backyard where we would play football, soccer, and baseball in the summertime. We never seemed to have a problem getting enough kids for a game. There were plenty around. Danny's Dad would play road hockey with us right up until the time he got smoked in the head with slapshot. He never played after that.

My passion for playing goal started early. During these road hockey games, I would play goal most of the time, but other kids liked to play goal too, so I had to swap out quite often. Even then, I never got the same rush scoring a goal as I did when I stopped one. The Frison's house was my second home, I would be there every day after school, and weekends as well. In the winter we played all the time. I would stay there while Ian and Eric went in for supper, and we'd play some more when they were done. I would go home well after dark, sometimes my Mom would drive over to get me because it was getting close to my bedtime. Keeping track of time was never as important as stopping shots.

It was around this time that I skated for the first time. My Mom signed me up for lessons at the rink which was about a fourty five-minute walk from school. By the time I got to the rink, the lessons were over and the kids were just skating on their own. I got my rented skates and stepped onto the ice for the first time ever. I immediately stumbled, put my hands down to stop me from falling over completely, and a girl skated over my fingers. Luckily, she was between strides and only cut me deep enough to barely draw blood. It stung like hell! I never wanted anyone to know I was hurt though, so I just wiped them on my jeans and tried again. I found it was easier to stay along the boards and push myself so I could glide. One of the parents who was watching through the chicken wire, (no plexiglass in those days, which tells you how old I am), said, "You're never going to learn that way!" He was right, but I was having fun. I think there were six lessons over six weeks, and then they tested you on what you have learned. Since I never made it to one lesson on time, I "failed most heinously", to quote Bill S. Preston. But I could skate a little bit. It would take me probably half an hour to get all the way around the rink, but I could do it having only fallen maybe twenty times. That would've been in grade 3 or 4 and was the last time I skated until Grade 7.

CHAPTER 2

The Move

When I was 10, my time with Mark Ferguson and the Frison Bros. started to come to an end when we moved a couple of miles away. For the first bit, I would ride my bike on Saturdays & Sundays to hook up with the old gang, but eventually I made new friends at my new school. Those trips became fewer and fewer until they just stopped altogether.

For most people, you just never know when you are going to meet the person that impacts your life more than any other. For me it was when I was 11. I made friends with this guy in my class named Kirk MacMillan. He was this kind of crazy guy, with an offbeat sense of humour, much like mine. We began hanging out quite a bit. It was Kirk who introduced me to this taller, red headed kid named Randy Aitken. Randall Buchanon Aitken was two years older than me, and he lived just up the street from Kirk. We stopped by the Aitken's house, and Randy was home with his older brother John. I was 11 and Randy was 13. We were just in the living room hanging out when I noticed that there were all sorts of trophies all over the place. Some belonged to Randy's Mom, Rose Aitken. She was an excellent ten pin bowler, and she won a lot of tournaments. She even represented Canada one time at a tournament in England. She would become my "other mother". She worked at Brentwood Lanes bowling alley which was down the hill from my house about a kilometer away. Randy had one older sister, Cheryl, who was a very good athlete in high school, and a couple of the trophies were hers. Others were John's, he was an amateur race car driver and raced all over the Pacific Northwest. Randy and I would be part of his pit crew, which really meant we just hung out at the race track. John was also a hockey player who played recreational hockey and was that older brother that every kid wanted to have. He was 22, but he loved hanging out with Randy and me. He would teach us things, take us places and listen to our stories. He treated us like equals, unlike most older brothers. And some of the trophies were Randy's. He played ice hockey. Which really made him special in my book. Up until then, I had never met a kid who played ice hockey. Not that I knew of anyway. He played in the Burnaby Minor Hockey Association. If I remember correctly, at that time he was a Bantam (age 13 & 14). In Bantam hockey nowadays "body checking" is not allowed, but back then it was. It was also the beginning of the Bobby Clarke and the Broad Street Bullies era, as well as the World Hockey Association. It was a tough game, played by tough men. The kids tried to emulate their favourite players as best they could. I don't remember if Randy had a favourite player, but Randy was a scorer. He scored a lot. He was a good skater and just seemed to have that knack for knowing where to be. Next to his family, I was his biggest fan. Randy had an absentee father. He never talked about him much. John and Cheryl didn't either, and I never really asked. I never knew his father's name or what he did for a living. I only knew that John was the father figure, and he was awesome. I only saw Randy's dad one time, at Randy's funeral when I was 14.

Randy and I became almost inseparable. We played all kinds of sports together, you name it, we played it. But mostly we played hockey. In the Aitken's living room, they had a big picture window. At night, they would close the curtains. That became the net. The goalposts were the TV to one side, and there was a chair on the other. We would all be on our knees. I would be in goal. John would be at the other end of the living room taking shots from about 6 feet away. Randy would be in front of the net trying to screen me, deflect shots, or score on the rebound. We used a ping pong ball and these little miniature hockey sticks that you could buy at Eaton's Department Store. We would spend a couple hours doing this until a TV show or hockey game came on that we really wanted to watch. "Emergency!" was our favourite. We always had to stop playing for Dixie McCall and John Gage.

When things got serious, we would go downstairs, I would put on the gear and we would do the same thing. Only down in the basement, there was a real hockey net. We used real sticks. And of course, the ever-present tennis ball. Every once in awhile we would even go outside and play in the street, but Randy lived halfway up Napier Street, and if Randy or John shot wide, the ball would end up a half mile up the road. Same thing if I let out a rebound that went past them. That was the downhill side, and the ball would just keep rolling and rolling. So that wasn't as much fun. We discovered if we played in the front yard on the grass, there were bushes that would stop the wide shots, so we played "grass hockey". After awhile we started wearing out the grass, so Mrs. Aitken put the kibosh on that activity.

My world centered around Randy. He went to a different school than me, but outside of that we were almost always together. After school I would go straight to his house and we would mostly play hockey, but there were a thousand other things to do at his house. I would sleep there on weekends, and during the summer, I would be there almost every night. They had a cot set up for me in Randy's room. Randy's family had a small dog named Lucky. Lucky would sleep in my sleeping bag at my feet. He was known for getting out of his harness. We would put his harness on to take him for a walk, then all of the sudden he wouldn't have it on anymore. He would do this thing where he would just kind of shake, like a dog does when he's wet, but he did it so fast, you couldn't tell how he was getting out of the harness. He was like the "Houdini" of the dog world. He wouldn't go anywhere, he'd just sit there and look at us, waiting for us to put the harness back on. It was like he did it just to show us that he could. He was a great dog, and he lived for about another year or so.

I would check in with my Mom every once in a while. My Mom was a worrier, but as long as she knew where I was, she was ok. She knew Randy's Mom because my Mom was a bowler as well, and she knew If I wasn't home, I was with Randy. He was my best friend, and it was always going to be that way.

I watched so many of Randy's hockey games, I couldn't even guess how many. But I only knew a couple of the players. One in particular I watched a lot. Tye Fitzsimmons. I really don't know why I had such an interest in watching him. I mean, he wasn't a goalie, but he was a smaller kid like me, and he was a really good player. The thing I remember most about him is, he was absolutely fearless on the ice. Remember, Bantam hockey had hitting. And punching, and pushing and shoving, and wrestling. Not too many fights as I remember, because if you fought, you would get kicked out of the game. If you fought someone in the third period, you would be suspended for the next game. Nobody wanted that. But it didn't matter to Tye how rough the game was. No matter what kind of brouhaha broke out, Tye would crawl out from underneath unscathed. Tye had what Randy and I called, his Ole' move. Tye would be skating down the wing with the puck and a player from the other team would take a run at him. Tye would stop on a dime, and the player would go for the big bodycheck and hit nothing, usually sending him off balance and into the boards. It was like watching a matador letting the bull run past him. Ole' Ole'. Tye would reappear in my life about ten years later.

As we got a little older, Randy and I started having other interests. Randy really liked girls, but I was not quite ready yet. But he liked them, so I said I liked them too. And we talked about them a lot. He introduced me to my first girlfriend, Tracy. Randy was her friend's boyfriend, but I don't remember her name. This would actually lead to the only time that Randy and I ever argued. It was over some teenage drama that I won't go into here. We didn't talk to each other for about a month, but eventually, things got smoothed over and we went on just like before, and we agreed never to let girls get in the way of our friendship ever again.

Around this time, I was in Grade 7 and had turned 12. Funny how today parents are hesitant to let their kids walk anywhere by themselves. In 1974 it wasn't like that. I usually walked home from Randy's house by myself at 8:30 when it was dark. I never gave any thought that there would be any danger. It only took me maybe ten or fifteen minutes to walk from Randy's house to mine. This one night I was walking home on Curtis Avenue, which is a pretty busy street most of the time. I had to walk down a pretty big hill to get to Holdom Avenue where I lived. I could access the back yard by turning onto a side street about halfway down the hill and then turning again into a back alley which led to our back yard. As I was approaching the side street, I heard somebody behind me so I turned and looked. It was a man and he was walking about 40 yards behind me. I couldn't really make out his features because the streetlight was behind him and all I could see was his silhouette. I really didn't think anything untoward was going to happen. Nobody ever told me that there were predators around. I heard the guy start running. He ran right up behind me and I thought he was just going to run right past, but he got close enough and just grabbed me and lifted me up. At the same time, he put his hand over my mouth so I couldn't yell out. He took me across the street where there was a pitch and putt golf course. At any time, a car could've come along and he would've been busted, but luck was not on my side this night. He took me far enough into the trees to where nobody could see us. He pushed me onto my back, put tape over my eyes, and then took my pants off and began to molest me. It lasted maybe about ten minutes. He didn't rape me or harm me in any way. He asked what my name was and I told him Randy. He asked where I lived and I pointed in the completely wrong direction and said "over there". He told me that he knew my name and where I lived and that if I told anyone about it, he would find me and hurt me. I knew that I had given him bogus information, but it scared me enough that I didn't tell anyone. I got home and acted normally. It took a couple of days but eventually I told Randy. I didn't want him to feel guilty because I was walking home from his house. I told another friend of mine as well and eventually the truth got out. I came home one day and my mom asked me about it. I told her what happened but I was scared that he was going to come and hurt me if anyone found out. My mom assured me that that wasn't going to happen and called the police. A couple of detectives came over to my house and I had to tell them everything that happened and where. In the meantime,

Randy was really mad. He wanted to go out and find the guy and "lay the boots to him". I don't think John found out until much later. I don't remember ever talking to him about it. After "the incident", when I was at Randy's house, he would walk me halfway home and then I would run the rest of the way. The school put out a warning that there was a child molester in the area and that parents should be vigilant. Even with the warning there was another kid in my class who fell victim to this creep. As I remember it, it took about a month or two to catch the guy. The other kid in my class and I had to testify against him. We were brought to the court the night before the trial and shown exactly what was going to happen. They had an extra charge against the guy because of his threat to me. On the day of the trial, we showed up at court. Just before we went in, the detective came out and told us that the guy had decided to plead guilty. Peter Alan Holman pleaded guilty to eight counts of child molestation and was sentenced to two years in Oakalla prison and then five years of probation. Something like this could really mess a kid up, but Randy helped me through it. He told me not to be scared of people and that we were going to grow and become stronger so that nobody is going to ever mess with us again. I had a good support system at home and my mom made sure that I was ok, and I was. I got over it pretty quickly, I was a little more wary of people walking behind me and I always made sure to get home quickly. But I totally forget about this incident in my life for years at a time, and I credit Randy with that. He just had this way of instilling confidence and he was my protector. I think of it now as "just something that happened". I don't let it affect me in any way. If I did, it would mean letting Randy down, and that just won't stand.

A couple of years later, Randy was playing Midget (ages 15-16) hockey. He would be 15 and I was 13 at this time. He scored 50 goals that year, and started getting interest from some junior teams. He was really excited. I remember telling him that I thought he was going to make it to the NHL. He said he thought so too. That summer he started not feeling very well. He couldn't leave the house because he was in a lot of pain, and he would throw up every now and then. I went over to his house quite a bit, but we would usually just watch TV or play board games. He taught me how to play chess and blackjack. After a couple of weeks, he had lost so much weight that he had to go into the hospital. Randy was a big kid, he was close to 6 feet and normally about 160 pounds, but he was probably down 20 pounds. He was in pretty good spirits, but he sure didn't like being in the hospital. Not that anyone does. He couldn't wait to go home. After a couple of weeks, he was feeling better and was allowed to leave. We returned to our normal activities somewhat. He got tired pretty easily and spent a lot of time on the couch. Then, not long after, he had to go back into the hospital. He was really sick this time. When I went to see him, he was laying on the bed and his eyes were closed. His mom whispered in his ear that I was there. He didn't open his eyes, but he kind of rolled over onto one side away from me and told me to feel his bed. I felt where he had been laying and it was totally soaked with sweat. I told him that was gross, and I wiped my hand off on my pants. He smiled. He thought that was pretty funny. He was always getting me to do stuff like that. One time, he had a job delivering sales flyers to apartment buildings. We were on the 3rd floor of this one place. We had delivered to every apartment, and were going to get on the elevator to leave and go to the next one. We were getting kind of restless, so we figured we would go home and play hockey. We decided to throw the remaining flyers down the garbage chute. There were quite a few left over, and Randy started throwing them down. He got the idea for me to go down to the 2nd floor, and stick my hand in the chute to try to catch some flyers on their way down. I thought that was a great idea, so I ran down one floor and went to the chute. I told Randy I was ready and a few flyers came down and hit my hand, but I didn't catch any. I told him to try again, and all I felt was this SPLAT. He had hawked a loogie right into the middle of my palm.

Nobody ever told me what was wrong with Randy. Just that he was sick and that he would get better eventually. During his second stint in the hospital, I didn't see him as often as the first time he was in there. After the sweat feeling incident, the next time I saw him, he was sitting up and joking around with his family. He said he'd had an operation. I remarked that he looked way better, and he said he was feeling better. Not long after that he got out of the hospital and went home. None of his clothes fit because he had lost so much weight, but he seemed to be back to his normal self. Again, we returned to our normal activities. Randy started to gain his weight back, but he was losing his hair. If you pulled on it, it would just come right out. He said it was because of the medicine he had to take. I didn't think much about it, but I thought it was really weird that he was going to have to wear a wig. He was adamant that his hair was not red, that it was auburn, so he wanted an auburn wig. I didn't even know there was a difference between red and auburn. I was just glad to have my friend back. As the summer wore on, things got more and more back to normal. We had our hockey games in the basement and living room. September rolled around and Randy wasn't allowed to play ice hockey yet because of the operation he'd had. We went to the rink and watched his team play a few times. This one game, we were watching Randy's team play and we were sitting behind the penalty boxes. There was the ever-present chicken wire in this rink. We could hear everything that was being said on the ice, and vice versa. At this point I should tell you that not everything John and Randy taught me was peaches and cream. It's during this time that I tried smoking, drinking alcohol, and swearing. A whole lot of swearing. The smoking and drinking never took hold, but my wife will tell you, to this day the swearing has never left me. Drives her nuts. Back to the game; it's me, Randy, and about 5 other teenagers. The referee called a penalty on Randy's team, and when he came to the time keepers bench to give the penalty, he's about 20 feet away from us. Randy and the other kids started chewing him out, "Terrible call ref!", "What're ya looking at? Are we even watching the same game?", "How much have they paid you?" Then, poetically, I pipe in at the top of my lungs, "YOU'RE BLIND, YOU FUCKIN' QUEER!!" The timekeeper turned around and ripped into me. I felt a little embarrassed, but Randy and his friends were laughing so hard they couldn't breathe. Their laughing drowned out anything the timekeeper had to say. We were all holding our stomachs, laughing as hard as humanly possible. I don't think I've ever told that story until now.

Randy's team was good, and they won a lot of games. They had a goalie named Rick Egerton, (pronounced EDGEurton). The guy was good, really good, actually. I enjoyed watching him play. The big news that fall was that the Egerton's were going to Hawaii, and they were bringing Randy along. What a lucky guy, I thought at the time. He was gone for a week or two, and when he came back, he showed me all the pictures he had taken during his trip. He had an awesome time. They went to a Luau, saw Diamond Head and Waikiki, and did all the touristy stuff. Randy even had a lei in his luggage that he gave to me.

Not long after, Randy went back into the hospital. I wasn't concerned. I figured he'd be there for awhile, and when he got home, we would continue on as usual. To my everlasting regret, I didn't go to see him. He had been in the hospital a few weeks when one Sunday morning, I went bowling down at Brentwood Lanes with two of my friends. Mrs. Aitken wasn't working that day. Sometimes she would let us bowl for free, and I was hoping that she would be there so I could ask her how Randy was doing. She usually worked Saturday Nights, but sometimes she would be there on Sundays as well. When walking home from the bowling alley, we had to climb up this big hill. Holdom Hill. It was a real thigh burner. We always dreaded it, and wished someone would come and give us a ride. On this particular day, my Mom drove up as we were about to crest the hill. Excited, we approached the car. My Mom asked me to get in, but asked my friends to stay outside. I got in, and I could tell right away that she had something serious to tell me. She couldn't say anything at first, and then finally, "Randy died last night."

At first, I didn't react. I just kind of let out an "ohh". I was definitely sad, but not crying. Looking back, I think I was in shock. She asked if I wanted to come home with her. I told her no, that I wanted to walk with my friends. I got out of the car, and she drove off. My friends, Mike and Dennis, both knew Randy through me. And they went to the same school as he did. I gave them the news, and we walked to my house talking about him. I thought it was weird that I wasn't crying, and I thought that maybe it wasn't going to bother me that much and I was going to be ok. As I walked up the front steps to my house, it all kind of dropped on me like a ten-ton weight. I started tearing up as I walked in the door, and it grew as I walked to the couch in the living room. By the time I sat down, I was in full sobbing mode. I don't remember Mike and Dennis leaving. I just remember holding my stomach and crying like I was never going to stop. "It's not fair," was all I could say.

To say that I was devastated would be the understatement of the century. Randy had died of stomach cancer, and I couldn't fathom it. Randy was, and then he wasn't. I didn't know he was going to die. I didn't know he was that sick. It just wasn't fair. He was going to play in the NHL, and now he's dead. There are no words to describe the depths of what I was feeling. I was 14 years old, and death had just kicked me in the nuts a thousand times. I cried a lot over the next six months or so. Sometimes my Mom would hear me at night and she would come into my room and we would talk about Randy and how much I missed him.

Randy's funeral took place on a beautiful sunny day, and the Aitkens had asked me to be a pallbearer at Randy's service, but I couldn't. Emotionally, I just wasn't up to it. My spirit was crushed and I was afraid I would break down and cry in front of everybody. My Mom and Marlene told me that it was a great honour to be a pallbearer, but I just couldn't do it. It was too much for me to bear. Cheryl had made sure that a seat was reserved for me, my Mom, and my sister Trish, (her and Randy were the same age and she was friends with some of his friends), right behind the pallbearers. We had the whole row to ourselves. There were a lot of people there, two or three hundred. Randy touched a lot of lives in his 16 years living on this earth.

There is a picture on the Aitken's mantle of Randy's last year actually playing hockey, from the year he scored 50 goals in Midget. He's in the back row, and he's laughing. Next to him is a kid named Greg Sallows. Randy said that Greg was pinching his bum while the photographer took the picture. Greg had died in a car accident not long before

Randy's passing. Such sadness. I learned much later that almost everyone knew that Randy was going to die. (I think that Randy knew. His Mom told me years later that a couple of times he had asked her "why me?" And that she didn't have an answer for him) That was the reason the Egerton's took him to Hawaii. Cheryl told me about how she had talked to Randy's doctor and how he had given her the bad news. They thought it best to keep it from me, because they didn't know how I would react. They thought I might go off the deep end and do something stupid. They were probably right.

Randy's death would influence me more than any other event in my entire life. Up to that point I had had it fairly good, meaning that I had never wanted for anything. My Mom was the sweetest person ever. Always smiling and doing everything for her kids. She lived for her kids. But life wasn't perfect. Far from it. My Dad drank too much and never really took much interest in us kids. I played lacrosse for one year when I was in grade 6, the only game he came to was played at Burnaby Winter Club. He only came because the arena had a bar. I looked up during the game a couple of times and he wasn't even watching, he was turned sideways, drinking beer and talking to the person next to him. He wasn't abusive or anything, but he was extremely stubborn, opinionated, impatient, and not the easiest guy to like. My Dad and I didn't have the best relationship, but I learned fairly early that we were just different people. I wasn't like him, and I wasn't expected to be. He never saw me play hockey, not once. It just didn't interest him. My Dad and I made our peace later in life, when I learned that he raised his kids the same way that his father raised him and his siblings. After Randy's passing, I realized that I had been taking life for granted and now I was going to have to accept that things were what they were, and I wasn't going to change anything if it was impossible to change. Life itself was a lottery win, and death was part of the package. If it could happen to Randy, it could happen to me. I decided that I was never going to worry about anything. My life could end at any time, and I was going to live every day as if it were my last, because you just never know. I was going to be nice to people, and I was going to be a little bit selfish. I was going to be happy and keep myself that way, no matter what. Since that day, every time I wake up, I thank whatever higher power is at work for giving me the day. Life is what you make it. And life does go on. A pretty heavy realization for a fourteen-year old. I would now forever have a guardian angel watching over me, and I wasn't going to dishonour his memory by being miserable. To this day, I still think about Randy a lot. I remember his laugh, and the way he walked. I remember him scoring goals and that he used to drive his mom crazy asking her for money. He wouldn't stop until she gave in, and she always gave in, eventually. Mrs. Aitken, my other mother, passed away from breast cancer in 1999. I hope that Randy was there to greet her when she crossed over. Sometimes Randy still appears in my dreams, he's just like he always was. Smiling and laughing. He had this cackle that was infectious. I couldn't help but laugh whenever he laughed. I love the guy, and I miss him. I always will.

CHAPTER 3

And the Band Played On

In the ensuing years, I guess John needed to fill the void in his life. After Randy died, he was lost. I heard him say a couple of times that he felt like killing himself. Thank God he didn't. I don't think I could've survived losing them both. After some time had passed and the pain had subsided somewhat, I guess I became the surrogate little brother. He took me to so many places, like movies and golfing. I still remained a member of his pit crew, and he took me everywhere he went racing. We went bowling, to Canucks games, baseball games, lacrosse games, BC Lions games, we went to shoot pool, you name it. It was kind of a symbiotic relationship, we needed each other. He had this habit of calling people "peckerhead" when they pissed him off. Somebody would do something that he didn't like, and he would say "peckerhead jerkenstein." That always made me laugh.

All through my high school years, I continued to play street hockey. We had a regular game every Friday night. The father of one of our group members was a pastor in the United Church, and the Church had a gym in the basement, so we gathered every week for a game. We also played on weekends at the tennis courts. The courts where we played had an added bonus, there were floodlights so we could play at night. And the sight of a bunch of teenagers playing ball hockey kept away any pesky tennis players. Also, during this time, the equipment we used got more and more like regular hockey equipment. Gone were the foam pads and winter coats. And we graduated from the tennis ball to the dreaded hockey ball. Most of us had part time jobs, or paper routes so we had some disposable income. I bought my first set of pads and gloves second-hand from other people. We would find other pieces from various sources, (stealing them was not out of the question). I would buy my sticks from Collegiate Sports in Brentwood Mall. A girl that I knew worked there, and she would give me a discount. I also got my first mask. It was a Jacques Plante special. It was maybe 3/8ths of an inch thick and only covered my face. When you got hit by the hockey ball, it would still leave a mark, but it didn't feel like you were going to die. If a ball came at me and I turned my head, it would hit me in the ear. Ouch! I learned pretty quickly not to do that.

My passion for the sport grew and grew. I thought about the game day and night. Always looking for ways to get better. I'm about 15 at this time, and I'm dedicated to the goalie position now. No more playing out. One guy in our group was an actual hockey prodigy. Lawrence Duke was a big kid, probably 6 feet and 200 pounds and was getting attention from junior teams. He would always want to take shots on me before the game began. And man, could he shoot. He had more velocity than anyone I had faced up to that point. And he could make the ball do the craziest things. At any given time, it could curve left or right, up or down, or even corkscrew. I had to focus hard and follow the ball right into my body. Every once in awhile, he would hit me in the head. If you lost your focus, even for a nanosecond, there were consequences. During the games was a little different.

He would shoot from everywhere, even from in front of his own net. The ball danced so much, it was always 50/50 if you stopped it or not. He was the best player among us. He went on to play Junior "A" hockey, and then he got a scholarship to a university in the U.S. and even played a little pro hockey.

Another guy I went to high school with who wasn't part of our group, was Ken Kinney. Ken was an actual ice hockey goalie, and he was very good. He was a year younger than me, so our paths only crossed occasionally. Despite that, we knew each other and were always friendly. When we played road hockey against each other, I would watch him like a hawk. I learned to use my stick to stop shots instead of my feet from Ken. I was forever getting bruised toes and insteps until I got this valuable piece of information. Ken was a cocky kid and he had a right to be. He went on to be a Junior "A" goalie, and I think he even got an NHL tryout. He won the Allan Cup with the Whitehorse Huskies in 1993, a painful subject for me that will come up later in this narrative. When I graduated from high school, Ken signed my yearbook as follows: "To a good goalie, from a better one." Like I said, Ken was cocky. He recently passed away from cancer after 28 years as a firefighter. R.I.P Kenny, you were indeed, a better goalie.

After I graduated from Alpha Secondary school in 1979, our same group of people were still doing the same things. The Friday night church game, the weekends at the tennis courts. It never got old. At least not for me. All I wanted to do was stop shots. I played whenever I could. Of course, partying was a major enterprise when we weren't playing. But that's another story for another time. I had a girlfriend at the time, Ruth. She was my first serious girlfriend. She taught me how to kiss. Ruth's parents were an odd couple. Her mother was seriously religious, but her father wasn't religious at all. He was just seriously serious. I spent a lot of time at their house and they were very accepting of me. Ruth had five brothers and sisters and they were religious too, except for her oldest brother, Bruce, who was kind of a hippy. Her parents didn't laugh much. Her father was a large man, and he was very intimidating. We were watching a variety show one night and a standup comedian was performing. It was just Ruth, her parents and I in the room. I have an offbeat sense of humour, to say the least, and sometimes things that aren't funny to anyone else will strike me directly on the funny bone. Well, this comedian was doing a bit about "pronouncing people dead". "How do you pronounce someone dead? Is it like an umpire coming over to you, pointing down at you and yelling, "Youuuuuurrrrrrrr DEAD!!". Like I said, not that funny to anyone else, but it hit me like a load of whoopie cushions. I burst out laughing and could not stop. I couldn't breathe. Ruth's mother was sitting in the chair knitting and just shaking her head. Her father was scowling at me. Their reaction just made me laugh harder. I was practically in convulsions. Ruth had to lead me out of the house. We broke up not long after.

Chapter 4

Get Some Skates Kid

In the spring of 1980, the New York Islanders won the Stanley Cup, beating the Philadelphia Flyers in 6 games. Bob Nystrom scored the Stanley Cup winning goal in overtime. I was happy, because finally someone other than the Montreal Canadiens won the cup. Despite rooting for the Canadiens when I was nine, I had grown to hate them. I was a diehard Vancouver Canucks fan by then. The Canadiens just kept on winning and winning. I was so tired of watching them win all the time. four straight years they won the cup without breaking a sweat. Little did I know that the Islanders were now on their way to doing the exact same thing. I would grow to hate them too. It was about a month after the Islanders had their first parade that I was over at the Aitken's house. John and I still hung out, but not as often as in the past. At this time, I was eighteen and had my own vehicle, (a 1969 Datsun pickup). We were discussing how happy we both were that the Montreal dynasty was seemingly over, when the topic of his hockey team came up. He was always playing in one beer league or another. (At one time he played in the N.H.L. The "Natural Hockey League") At this time he was playing on a team called the Burnaby Kings, and they were playing at the Columbian 4 Rinks. At one time, this was the largest indoor hockey arena in the world, and was even in the Guinness Book of World Records. As it turned out, the Kings were renting one of the rinks once a week, all summer long. Summer hockey was a new thing, all the other rinks became lacrosse rinks for the summer. John was telling me how terrible their goalie was. The guy's name was Lonnie. I don't remember his last name. John was telling me that the guy was the worst goalie he had ever played with. They had nicknamed him "Red Light Lonnie," because he would let in so many goals. He said that Lonnie was so short that shots would regularly hit him in the head and deflect into the net. One time John said that the puck had been shot into the corner and Lonnie went to go get it, fell down, and while he was trying to get up, the puck went up on edge and had such spin on it after it hit the boards, that it reversed itself and curved right into the net. John said Lonnie was like "Bad Luck Schleprock" of the Flintstones.

I asked John if he thought I could get a tryout. I had all the equipment, even if it was for road hockey. He said they were always trying to find goalies, as there weren't that many willing to give up their summer activities. They had played just the night before so I had a week to upgrade anything that needed it. Foremost, I had to buy a pair of skates. I mentioned earlier that I had skated in grade 3 or 4 and since then, I hadn't added to my experience very much. In grade 7 our class went ice skating regularly every 3 weeks. I remember Rhonda Huth skating with her arm crossed into our teacher's (Mr. McFarland) arm, so that their forearms were together, and holding hands, they both had gloves on, of course. Teachers pet. I tried my best, but skating did not come naturally to me, and I really wasn't all that motivated to get better. I could get around the rink, and I could reverse direction when the voice on the loudspeaker said to do so. Good enough.

Randy and I would go public skating sometimes. I was always asking him to teach me how to stop, but he never did. I would just skate into the boards. In high school, public skating was considered "uncool", so I didn't go. I wasn't the coolest kid around, but I didn't need anyone thinking I was "uncool".

So back to Collegiate Sports I go. My friend, Laurie Pecaric, showed me all the skates. I looked first at all the goalie skates, but they were all out of my price range. I decided to get a pair of Lange player skates. They had a hard, plastic outer shell, and I figured this would be enough protection for my feet. I figured wrong. So, the skate thing was all figured out, for now. I didn't have any money left to upgrade any more of my equipment. I had these old Cooper pads that barely covered my knee, and players hockey pants that had no protection for the inner thigh. Of course, I can't forget about the Jacques Plante special. You could rent goalie equipment at the rink, and I think that's what I did for my gloves and chest protector. It was like $5.00 to rent for a couple of hours, and I could afford that, so I was good to go.

When the time came, I went to John's house, and we went to the rink together. The rink was only a ten-minute drive from there. I couldn't contain my excitement. I was almost bursting out of my skin. I was eighteen, and I was actually going to be a real ice hockey goalie. The dream was alive. We walked into the dressing room, and I met Hugh, the man who ran the Kings. He introduced me to the other guys. Most had been friends with each other for years. There was Bruce Saarinen, Earl Berg, Wade Hawksworth, Ron Breidt, and a host of others whose names escape me. The only guy I knew other than John, was Andy McLean. He was a friend of John's who was an amateur race car driver as well, so I had seen him regularly at the racetrack. I was mostly listening to the banter when in walked Lonnie, the shitty goalie. He was quite a bit shorter than me with brown hair, cut in a military style. He walked into the room with the confidence of a man who was absolutely the best player he knows. He was cocky as fuck. I guess he was deluded into thinking he was a great goalie. He was an alright guy, but one of those people who just loved to talk about himself. He wasn't just the star of the team. He was the whole fuckin' galaxy.

Chapter 5

A Different World

I managed to figure out how to get my pads on over my skates, and then the rest of the equipment followed. The Zamboni took about ten years to get off the ice. The time came for me to make my debut. The definition of inauspicious is as follows: "showing or suggesting that future success is unlikely". Inauspicious doesn't even come close to describing my entrance to the game of ice hockey. When I stepped on the ice there was about a one-foot drop from the gate. I stepped down and tried to skate, but the equipment seemed like it weighed a ton and was toppling me over. The skates were not helping as there was no resistance under my toes. I fell over onto my hands and knees and needed help getting up. I'm sure the guys were all thinking that they got the one goalie in Vancouver who was worse than Lonnie. Once I got to my feet, I was able to get some bearings. I skated to the net and just stood in front of it while the others skated around doing their pregame routines. After about 5 minutes, someone brought a big 20-gallon plastic paint bucket out on the ice and dumped a bunch of pucks from it. Guys started grabbing pucks, skating in on net and shooting. I was stopping most of them, but then again, I don't think they were trying too hard to score. After about 5 minutes of this, everyone lined up just inside the blue line and started taking slapshots. There is a world of difference between a hockey ball and a puck. The puck is much heavier and it doesn't curve, twist or corkscrew like a hockey ball. The puck seemed to me to be moving almost in slow motion. "This is gonna be easy!" I thought. Then Bruce Saarinen took a shot. Bruce was a big guy, but he skated like he was a featherweight. The guy must've played some serious hockey. When he shot on me for the first time, he missed the net. Thank God. The puck hit the boards and went BOOM! I was just thankful he missed me or else I might've ended up the medical room. The puck came so fast it was just a tiny black blur. Holy shit… I'm gonna need better equipment! We went through the line a few times, Bruce being directly in front of me and right in line with the other net. It would go: Shot… Shot… Shot… Shot… BRUCE!!!… Shot… Shot… Shot. With the warmup over. The game was about to begin. Thank God Bruce was on my team. I couldn't have been more excited. To anybody watching it probably looked like what it was; a bunch of guys playing at the lowest level. But to me it was NHL caliber. I'd like to say I was awesome, but I wasn't. I was better than Lonnie though. I made some really good saves, but let in some real stinkers. Afterwards, Lonnie said, "I don't feel guilty about any of those goals I let in. Gary Smith wouldn't have stopped those." The guy, most definitely, was in major denial. I, on the other hand, felt completely guilty about the ones I let in, and Gary Smith would've undoubtedly stopped those.

Wade Hawksworth was my first breakaway save. He came in and made a deke, to which I just laid down in the direction he went and he hit me somewhere on my body. Great save. The next time he got a breakaway, he made the same move. So did I. He just waited for me to lay down, and then just shot it in the top of the net. Not so great. Guess I was going to have to learn how to play in this brand-new world.

Chapter 6

The Mask

Over the next few weeks, I started to learn. I learned that my equipment was completely inadequate. After playing I would feel like one big bruise. And I absolutely had to get some goalie skates, or it was only a matter of time before I broke some toes. That was first on the list. Back to Laurie I went to try on some goalie skates. I picked the cheapest ones. Instead of buying better equipment; I just bought more second hand stuff and added it to what I was already wearing. I bought another chest protector and wore it over top of the one I bought previously. I had a pair of football pants that I got from Randy when he played high school football. I taped some volleyball knee pads to the inner thighs and I wore them underneath my hockey pants. I bought some real goalie knee pads that protected the knee and the lower thigh. There was always an opening between the bottom of your pants and the top of your pads when you went to make a save on your knees. If you got a good shot there, you would have trouble walking for awhile afterwards. There's another spot between the top of your blocker and elbow that would paralyze your hand if you got hit there. It would go away after a few minutes, but again, it would be sore for awhile and you wouldn't be able to hold onto your stick. I added little bits of padding everywhere that

I could. Volleyball knee pads were the best for this, and I put them everywhere. In the dressing room, guys would laugh at me and say that they couldn't tell if I was playing hockey or volleyball when I was getting dressed.

After that first time playing on ice, it became readily apparent that my Jacques Plante special wasn't going to cut it. I was lucky that I never took a head shot during that game. I probably would've ended up in the hospital. I tried to find a better one in the stores, but they only sold helmet and cage combos, and I wanted a mask. Just like the ones the NHL'ers had. I talked to Ken Kinney, and he told me that THE GUY to go to was Vic Lemire. Vic had played some junior and university hockey and then came home and started a goalie school that was very popular with all the goalies in town, (apparently). He made masks as a side business, but I had never heard of him. I gave him a call and asked him how much it would be to have a mask made for me. He said $155.00. I coughed into the phone and nearly passed out. The most I had paid for any equipment, other than my skates, was $25.00. When I stopped coughing, he asked me how much my head was worth to me. I told him exactly $155.00. Thus, I made an appointment to get my mask made.

Little did I know that getting a mask made was quite the process. I showed up at Vic's house at the appropriate time and he led me down into his laboratory. It must have been Igor's day off. He had me lay down on a table and put water then Saran Wrap on my face. He then stuck two straws into my nostrils and told me to breathe normally. My initial thought was, "Is there any other way to breathe?" I did the best I could, and he started putting plaster of paris all over my face. When he was finished, I had to lay there for 20 minutes breathing as "normally" as I could. After suffering through that process, he gently removed the straws, and the hardened shell that was the end result. When he took the straws out of my nose, I was finally able to breathe normally. He said it would take about two weeks until the mask was ready. I paid the man and left the house. It was a long two weeks. I decided not to risk my life and rented a helmet and cage for the next two games.

The day came for me to get my new mask, and I was very excited as I had picked the Gary Bromley design. Gary "Bones" Bromley played for the Canucks and had what I thought was the coolest mask ever. It was painted like a skeleton head and was really freaky. When Vic handed me my mask, I couldn't believe how heavy it was. It was plain white, and it weighed twenty times what the Jacques Plante special weighed. It also came with a back plate to protect the back of your head, which the Jacques Plante special didn't have. I put it on. I felt at first like John Hurt in "Alien" when the hand-shaped creature was attached to his face. But it fit like a glove. Just a few adjustments of the straps, and I was good to go. It covered almost my whole head which would take some getting used to. He said it would be a little hotter than the other one. I asked him what it would feel like when I got hit with a good shot. He said that I would feel pressure, and it might snap my head back a little. He also mentioned that there shouldn't be any bleeding as the mask is designed to spread the pressure outward, but that I would feel wide awake and would get a wicked adrenaline rush. You could just tell the high quality of the thing and I still have it to this day, fourty years later. Game day came. It was a really hot day, and I was too excited to go to John's house. I went straight to the rink. I think I was like two hours early. The group ahead of us needed a goalie so I got dressed. I had forgotten my jersey at home so one of the guys lent me one. I headed out onto the rink with my new mask. I felt a little claustrophobic with it on, and it felt so heavy on my head. I went into the net and immediately started sweating like a rock star. I sweat easily to begin with, and with the new mask, I felt like I was in a blast furnace. But it gave me a sense of confidence. Before, when someone was taking a shot, (especially Bruce), I was so worried about getting hit in the head that I couldn't help but flinch. But with the new mask, I never felt the need.

The guys were taking a break when John arrived at the rink. One of the guys recognized him and called him over. Him and John were chatting through the chicken wire, (no glass yet). I skated over and said, "Hi John!" I could tell he didn't recognize me, he just said, "How ya doin?'" I took my mask off, and he said, "Oh, it's you! New mask?" "Yeah, I just got it!" I said. "Cool!" he replied.

We played our game, and then went to the bar. I was only 18 at the time and bar age was 19. I guess I looked old enough because no one ever said anything. I would sit there and drink Coke, and shoot the shit with the other guys. Lonnie never came up, I guess he didn't want to socialize with players who weren't up to his level. Sometimes we would stay until the bar closed. I didn't have a job at that point, so what the hell? Why not? The next week we played again, and I hadn't taken my hockey equipment out of the bag. I didn't know that it wouldn't dry on its own. My t-shirt and socks and everything else were still soaking wet from the previous week. I had figured that it would just dry itself. I couldn't have been more wrong. I started to put it on, and it was wet, clammy and cold and smelly. I remarked to the guy sitting next to me that there can't be anything worse than putting on wet sweaty hockey equipment. He said he thought the only thing that could possibly be worse would be putting on somebody else's wet sweaty hockey equipment. After that I learned to take my stuff out of the bag, so it could dry and then wash it every few times you used it. Somebody gave me a can of Lysol and told me to spray the inside of my bag every week, so bacteria wouldn't build up. Life lessons, I guess.

That was the way it went for that summer. August came, and I was getting better. I was still no great shakes, but I was way better than Lonnie. Lonnie didn't know it yet, but talk in the bar was the Kings were going to go with two goalies, and Lonnie had always made it clear he wouldn't sit. Meaning he would never be a backup. He played every game or none of them. He thought he was Glenn Hall.

Finally, the time came. The 1980/81 season was approaching and a decision had to be made. Hugh called Lonnie and told him the Kings were going to go with two goalies. "You know I won't sit?" Lonnie repeated. Hugh said he understood and the two agreed to part ways. Lonnie would find another team to stink for. Our paths would cross a couple of times at the rink. He never showed any animosity towards me, which you have to give him credit for, but he was still a terrible goalie.

Chapter 7

I'm on a Real Team

Ron Breidt had played forward the entire summer. I had no clue that he was a goalie. Not until the season started and he walked in with his goalie gear. He had never said a word, (and we had talked quite a bit). He had never offered any advice or spoke at all about being a goalie. I had known for awhile that the team was going to go with two goalies, but I figured it would be me and Lonnie. Despite his protests, I figured Lonnie would give in and split time with me. To my surprise it was going to be me and Ron, and Ron was a great guy. Ron played the first game, and I was happy to be on the bench. The team we were playing were called, The Smokers, and they were pretty good. We were not. Our guys were gamers, but talent wise, we just didn't stack up. Playing over the summer there were no referees, no faceoffs, no fans, no time clock, no penalties, no offsides or icing. Now there were all of these. It was all so "official". I couldn't believe I was playing real hockey; on a real team. It seemed like a dream. Of course, we lost. We would lose a lot over the next two seasons.

After that first game, we had a week until the next one; which I would play in. I was already nervous. The week lasted about a month, and finally it was time for me to make my ice hockey league debut. And wouldn't you know it; we were playing, The Canadiens. The irony was not lost on me. This was the team I had rooted for when I was nine, and now I'm playing the first game of ice hockey in my life against their namesake. The Canadiens were a mid-level team in our twelve-team league. The Flyers, Islanders and Smokers were the three top teams. We were close to the bottom, with The Malones, The Chargers, and The Cyclones.

I was so nervous, the butterflies in my stomach felt like a swarm of locusts. I had read that Glenn Hall threw up before every game, and now, I could understand why. Opening faceoff and the game was on. They scored on their first two shots. I stopped the third one and actually made a really good save on the fourth one. After that, it's all a blur. We lost something like 5-2 or 6-2. They must've had about 30 shots, I figure, so I stopped most of them. I wasn't happy we lost, but I had a blast. It was so much fun. I couldn't think of doing anything else. I could've played forever. For everyone else, it was old hat. For me, there was nothing like it. I was hooked like a junkie on heroine.

We got back to the dressing room, and everyone was acting like we had won the game. I didn't get it, we had lost, badly. They were all like, "yeah, but with Lonnie in net we would've lost 15-2. At least you kept us in the game." I guess nothing compares with low expectations.

Over the rest of the season, I bonded with my teammates. They were all good guys, and we hung out a lot. I was the youngest by at least 5 years, but it didn't seem to matter. We would all go to the bar after games or out for pizza and have a great time. The games seemed to be secondary to everyone except me. I lived it and loved it. Nothing else even mattered. It's all I wanted to do. I played as often as I could, anywhere I could, and with whoever I could. And if I couldn't play, I went to Public Skating. All my extra padding seemed to be doing the job. I would go a few games between bruises and was getting used to my mask. At this point though, I still hadn't taken a good headshot. That changed when I got a phone call to play some pickup hockey with guys I didn't know. It was at a different rink. I showed up, got dressed and took the warmups. Nobody seemed to be any better than anyone on the Kings so I had thought to myself; "No problem". There was this one guy who most definitely was the worst player out there. He was what we call an "ankle burner". An ankle burner is someone who can't stand up straight on their skates, and their feet kind of splay out, which makes it look like their inside ankles are going to drag on the ice. About halfway through the game, this guy has the puck coming into our zone to my left. He gets to about the outer faceoff circle, which was 35 or 40 feet from me, and I'm waiting for the inevitable soft shot. I'm guessing all the stars had aligned in just the right way, because the guy winds up and lets go an absolute cannon right to my forehead. I saw a white flash, then I went deaf. Vic never told me how loud it would be when you get hit with a slap shot. After it hit me, the puck went straight up and hit the rink ceiling. I got the adrenaline rush that he told me about, but the deafness was a surprise. It lasted maybe 15 seconds, and then my hearing started to come back quickly, replaced by a ringing in my ears. The ringing subsided a couple of minutes later. I picked up my carcass and went to the bench as I had to go sit down for a while. So, now I knew what it was like to take a real headshot. Not fun. But it was the price I would have to pay to play the game I loved.

About half way through the Kings season, I started to show some real improvement. Up until then, I was pretty much all reflex and zero technique. I had a habit of falling backwards. A guy would come in over the blue line and wind up for a slap shot, and I would be laying on my back, waving my hand in the air. One of the referees had said to me: "You know… technically, you're not that great. But you sure are fun to watch!" I was keeping the team in games they had no right to be in. I was still letting in the odd stinker, but they were getting fewer and farther between. I was getting advice from Ron as well. He was a very fine goaltender. I watched him when he was in the net to see what he did in different situations, and he would describe to me ways to play. For instance, how to see around players standing in front of the net, or how to watch the play when it's behind the net. I soaked it all in like a sponge. Our team even won a few games, always against the lower level teams in our league, but what the hell! A win is a win! I think we won 5 games that first year out of the 35, or 40, that we played.

About three quarters of the way through the season, Ron decided he didn't want to play goal anymore. He wanted to play out. For the life of me, I couldn't understand why anyone would want to play out. But, what the hell? I was going to be able to play every game from now on. I would still have Ron around acting as my soundboard. This was a win-win situation.

It was during this time that a situation arose during a game that I had never seen before or since. Wade Hawksworth was one of our better players. We were playing one of the lower level teams that were at the bottom of the standings with us. The play was in the attacking zone, and the puck was in the corner. For some reason, the goalie skated out of his net to go get it. The only problem was there was one of their players and one of our players already there. Our guy had gotten the puck first and passed to Wade who was in front of the net, and the goalie had fallen down. So, there's Wade, who has the puck on his backhand, inside the crease, and in front of a gaping wide-open net and nobody within twenty feet of him. Then, he backhands the puck over the net! The puck actually went out of the rink! Makes you wonder if sometimes the laws of physics can be broken. The other thing I remember about Wade was he had a hair trigger temper. I'm pretty sure he led our team in penalty minutes. This one time, Wade was trying to keep a guy from getting to the front of our net for a screen. They were battling off to the side of the net about ten feet from me. The guy gave Wade a pretty good slash with his stick, and Wade dropped his gloves and punched the guy right in the face. The only problem was, the guy was wearing a cage. Wade got kicked out for fighting that time. After the game, in the dressing room, Wade showed us the criss cross marks on his hand. How he didn't break any bones, I'll never know. When he punched the guy, you could hear it down the block. Another time, we were playing the Smokers, and they had a really good goalie. This guy had really long hair, and he really liked to wander and play the puck. He was good at it too, really smooth. Sometime late in the game, the goalie had the puck and was skating out of his net. Wade skated in on him and tried to get the puck, but the guy made a move and passed the puck up to one of his teammates. Wade stumbled, fell down and slid past him. I guess Wade didn't like the fact that he got sucked out by a goalie, so as this goalie was skating backwards returning to his crease, Wade came up behind him and cross checked him to the ice and jumped on him. In hockey, the goalie is untouchable, the consequences of even looking at the goalie the wrong way can be dire. Everybody knows this. Everybody except Wade, apparently. The play was going up the ice and all the players with it, unaware of what was happening behind them. The Smokers immediately left their bench, all of them, and made a beeline for Wade. When one bench clears, the unwritten rule is for the other one to clear so that everything is even. So about one second after the Smokers clear their bench, the Kings bench clears. All of their guys are after Wade who is wind-milling their goalie on the ice. All the players who were on the ice finally realized what was going on and paired off. It was absolute bedlam. In the four rinks, each rink is designated a colour. We were on the Blue Rink at the end of the building. The Penalty Box bar looked down onto this rink. The other rinks in order are the Red, Gold and Green. Someone who was watching our game goes running down past each rink yelling, "there's a brawl on blue, there's a brawl on blue!!!" On the ice, everything is chaos. Everyone is fighting. It is usually tradition for the two goalies to fight each other during a bench clearing brawl, but since their goalie was at the bottom of a dogpile and neither team had a backup goalie, I got off easy. I just stood there watching. The referees, of which there were only two, would pry two guys apart, put one in the penalty box and the other would be sent to the dressing room. Since they didn't want any other fights to start, they kept sending the Smokers players to the dressing room and our players to the penalty box. They had to use both penalty boxes. It took about twenty minutes for everything to settle down, and when we looked around, there were about 300 people watching. There were people all around the boards, including all the Smokers who had been kicked out, and players from other rinks. There were people in the stands behind the rink, and everyone in the bar had their noses pressed up against the windows. I had to laugh. My first bench clearing brawl, and I had the best seat in the house.

I played the rest of the season and kept improving. My skating was getting stronger but was still my weakest point. I still relied too heavily on my reflexes, (which were very good, but not great), and not enough on technique. I could've really used some coaching, but I couldn't afford to go to a goalie school like Vic's. So, I just watched. I watched every goalie I saw. Even the bad ones, because maybe they did one thing really well that I could incorporate into my own game. I watched and I learned. I got to recognize the different styles that goalies play. The Butterfly was one style, which Tony Esposito and Glenn Hall played. There were standup goalies; such as Pete Peeters and Ken Dryden. Goalies who played the puck a lot, like Gerry Cheevers, and goalies who were super aggressive like Mike Palmateer. Shot blockers; goalies who were just so big that the puck hit them most of the time. Guys who played on the goal line and relied on their reflexes were called "reflex" goalies, like Mario Lessard and Felix "*The Cat*" Potvin. I watched them all, as well as everyone I played with or against. I would keep what worked for me and discard the rest. Or if it didn't work at first, I would put it away in my memory bank, to come out at a later date, after I got better. I was like Johnny Five in *Short Circuit*: "More input, more input!".

In beer league hockey, everyone makes the playoffs, but not in 1981. Your team would have to qualify. Our league had two divisions of six teams each. You had to finish in the top four to qualify. We weren't even close. Our season was over near the end of March. However, there was a spring tournament that the 4 rinks held every year. It lasted until the end of May. You played once a week for six weeks in a round robin format, and then they would put you in a division with other teams that had similar records, and then you would have playoffs. Single knockout, which means; if you lose one game after the playoffs started, you're out. It was a lot of fun. Mostly because you had the chance to play teams you hadn't seen before. Teams from all over the lower mainland would participate. I can't remember what our record was, but I'm pretty sure we won at least a couple of games. During this tournament is when I got my first exposure to playoff hockey. We lost. Badly. I think it was like 12-1. Some team had sandbagged. They had lost most of their round robin games on purpose so they could get into a lower division's playoffs and win easily. Peckerheads. What some people won't do, just to win a trophy.

I said at the time that I was sorry we didn't win, but I was kind of glad it was over. I had played a lot and became a little burned out. Even at 19 years old, I needed a bit of a break. After a couple of weeks, the Kings began their summer hockey again, once a week at the 4 Rinks. It was mostly the same group with a few new additions. John was able to get Tod and Brett Sullivan to play. They were both friends of Randy's, and they were good hockey players. They were Toronto Maple Leaf fans, but other than that, they were good guys (settle down all you Leaf fans, I'm joking). We got a guy named Hank, I think he had a Swedish last name, but I can't remember it. He just walked into the dressing room one day and asked if we needed any players. He turned out to be a really good defenseman. An offensive defenseman, which we didn't have. And a few others also joined our ragtag team.

Chapter 8

A Rookie No More

The summer went on like the previous one. Ron went back in goal, which kind of pissed me off. I mean, make up your mind. Are you a goalie or not? For the summer, we needed two goalies so it was okay.

During one of our weekly games is when I got my first taste of actually playing against a real live, professional hockey player. He was skating on another rink and when their ice time ended, he came over and asked if he could skate with us. I don't remember his name, but he said he played for the New Haven Nighthawks of the American Hockey League. You could tell this guy was for real. He was so much better than everyone else, you couldn't help but see it. I was so intimidated and in awe of him, I couldn't think straight. He scored on me every time he shot the puck in my direction. It seemed like he wasn't even trying, which he probably wasn't. He could probably tell I was a newbie so he would only take wrist shots or snap shots. The puck would do this weird thing, it seemed like it was coming at me slow at first and then about halfway it would triple its velocity and zip right by me. I thought Bruce had a hard shot, (which he did), but this guy made Bruce's shots look like a baseball slow pitch. He only played that one time, and I never saw him again.

The summer ended, and the 1981/82 season was about to begin. We were playing in the same league against mostly the same teams. I was 19 and legally old enough to get into the bar. The bar personnel had finally caught me. One night, they asked to see my I.D., and I told them I didn't have any. I spent a couple of months of the previous season not going to the bar with my teammates. A sacrifice one must make. But now it didn't matter. I was legal and bring it on. The League was much the same with a few differences. New teams like The Colts, and The Golden Bears joined the league. Some new meat anyway. We had improved, and I had improved so I thought we would have a chance to challenge for a playoff spot. Ron again went to play out and left me to handle the goaltending duties. I had absolutely no problem with that.

In early September, I got a call from John Wiltsie. I had played against his team in an exhibition game during the summer. They were entering a team in a league in North Vancouver, and they were looking for a goalie. I said sure. (I hardly ever said no when it came to playing hockey). The team was called, Cottrell Forwarding. It was the company name that a few of the guys on the team worked for. We would eventually assume the name Buzzards, but it never really took hold. Everyone, including us, called the team Cottrell. John Wiltsie was a mountain of a man. He wasn't that tall, maybe 6 feet, but he was a good 260 pounds. He had a big beer belly but he was solid. He had a big bushy beard and a deep gravelly very loud voice. He was very intimidating, and his social skills could best be described as below average. He looked like a biker, but he wasn't. One time in the dressing room, John was sitting next to Greg MacDougall, who was an absolute neat freak. Greg liked to wash his gear between games and always had to have things clean and folded just so. John and Greg would be best described as Felix and Oscar times a thousand.

This particular night, the two of them were next to each other, Greg was already seated and had his bag open, and was starting to dress. John came in, sat down and opened his bag. He took out a few items and then exclaimed: "Holy fuck!", he then reached into his bag and grabbed something then threw it into Greg's bag exclaiming loudly, "Fucking cat shit in the bag again!" As you can imagine, Greg was absolutely disgortified (disgusted and mortified at the same time). But John was twice his size. Greg just stood up and went and grabbed a paper towel. He picked the evidence of the Wiltsie cat's indiscretion out of his bag and flushed it down the toilet. He then, without being discreet about it, grabbed all his stuff and moved across the room. John just laughed at him. Surprisingly, and despite his lack of couth, John was a very good hockey player. He definitely had some skills. His claim to fame was that he had played for Ralph Backstrom and the Chicago Cougars in the WHA as a goon. I can't find his name in the hockey database so I can neither confirm nor deny this. Maybe he played under a different name. John did have some secrets. About 5 years after I met him, John, his wife and child mysteriously dropped off the face of the earth, and nobody has heard from them since.

Cottrell had some good players. John Wiltsie, Eric Losch, Ed O'Leary, Mike Desmarais, Bruce Busby, Dave "Mad Dog" Watson. We also had Peter Wong, who worked at Cottrell and really just wanted to hang out with the guys. He could barely skate. He had these short little choppy strides, and it would take him probably 45 seconds to get from one end of the rink to the other. But he was a really funny guy and everyone liked him, so he would come out and they would spot him a few shifts a game. Somebody told me that Peter was driving a forklift on the dock located on Burrard Inlet. As he got off the forklift, he didn't engage the parking brake, and he knocked the shifter into reverse and the $50,000 forklift drove backwards right off the dock and into the inlet (being a forklift driver myself, this story is particularly funny). We also had Danny Lesko, who was going to be my backup goalie. That was cool because I never had a backup before. Danny was a late starter like me. I think he was 30 before he put on a pair of skates. He was not bad, but not good. Whenever he played, everyone tried a little harder to block shots and keep the play towards the opposite side of the arena. Despite that, Danny was a good guy, and I liked him. We had a very good team, compared to the rest of the league. The North Shore Intermediate Recreational Hockey League had 6 teams. We played on Friday nights. There were three ice times starting at seven o'clock; meaning all six teams played every Friday night. Our first game was against Larry's Sporting Goods. The hot rumour around the water cooler was that they were the team to beat. I think we won 4-3, I had probably the best game I ever played up to that point.

I was still improving, and between the two teams, I was playing a lot of games. The Kings were much improved but the problem was, so was the rest of the league. The teams that were beatable for us the year before, all of the sudden were beating us regularly. I was getting 40 or 50 shots a game. The guys were always joking that I should sue them for non-support. Anyway, the season for The Kings went on much like the season before. Not many wins. I think we had five again and a few ties. Most of the season for me was like a shooting gallery. In hindsight, it probably was the best thing for me. I had so many shots every night that I couldn't help but learn and improve. I had come light years from that nervous nellie who had started the previous season.

In stark contrast, Cottrell hardly ever lost. It was such a weird feeling when you come to the rink and expect to win.

It was something new for me. Dave "Mad Dog" Watson was a superstar. He scored at least one goal almost every game, sometimes two, three or even four. The guy was almost unstoppable. A bit of a nutbar, (he once got stabbed outside a nightclub), but man, could he play. We had other guys too. Eric Losch was a powerful skater and a real student of the game. He passed the puck as well as anyone and got a lot of assists (I found out later that Eric died in 2005 under very mysterious circumstances). Everyone else seemed to chip in when we needed it. And I was there holding the fort. I was having a great season and my confidence was growing. The North Shore News was a local newspaper, and they covered our games every week. I got some nice mentions in the paper, and they even had a picture of me making a save once.

The Kings finished last in the Burnaby league and missed the playoffs for the second straight year. Cottrell on the other hand finished 2nd in the league, and I got my first real playoff experience. Of the six teams in the league, only the top four made the playoffs. Guess who we had to play? None other than the Canadiens. It was a different team than the one in the Burnaby league. But hell, does every league have to have a team called the Canadiens? Is it some rule? Anyway, it was a best two out of three, and we won two-straight. I think the scores were 3-1 and 2-0. I allowed only one goal in two games. Pretty good for any goalie, and I was pretty proud of myself. The finals would be the next weekend, and I couldn't wait. It was going to be a best of five final. I was loving playoff hockey. Everything is just that much more intense. The adrenaline pumps a little harder, and you are a little more desperate to make that save.

The final was to be played over the next Friday and Saturday Nights. Then set to finish the following weekend. We had to play Larry's Sporting Goods. They had finished first in the league and were pretty much head and shoulders better than everyone else. We had beaten them the first game, but after that, I think we might've had one tie against them. They pretty much dominated everyone. Wednesday night I came down with the flu. "Not now," I thought to myself. But it was definitely a flu bug. Luckily it wasn't a stomach flu, just a fever, chills, feel-like-shit kinda flu. All Thursday, I stayed in bed and drank water. I tried to flush it out with fluids, like mom always told me. Then I wrapped myself in blankets and tried to sweat it out. Friday morning, I felt marginally better but not a lot. Game time came, and I felt quite a bit better. During warmups, I felt like I was looking through a wide-angle lens. I didn't take many shots. I figured I would save my energy, and if Danny had to play, he would've had a good warmup. I told him to be ready. I managed to be a good soldier and made it through the game, but we lost. I think it was 5-2. When Saturday rolled around, I was feeling better, but not 100%. Gametime came and again, we did our best, but they were just a better team. We lost 4-1 with an empty net goal. The next week was long, but I was still playing with the Kings in the spring tournament, and I managed to grab another game with another team I spared with. The flu bug wormed its way out of my system, and I was feeling pretty good when Friday came around, and I had a great game, even though the team only managed to score three goals. We won 3-2. We lived to fight another day! And then we were dead. Saturday came, and it wasn't even a game. They just decided to ramp up operations and toss us aside. 6-1 was the final. Men against boys. It would be the first of many times I would go to the finals and lose. Not a good feeling, in fact in the words of local DJ Willy Percy, "It sucks the royal."

About two weeks later, the NSIRHL had their one-and-only awards banquet. I knew I hadn't won the best goalie award. It went to the team with the best Goals Against Average, and that was Larry's Sporting Goods. I never talked at all with the other players in the league, other than to chirp them during the games, and I didn't do very much of that anyways. I found it to be distracting and took away from my performance. Because of that I didn't know anyone who wasn't on my team. All the guys on our team were there, Dave "Mad Dog" Watson had won the league scoring title and was going to get a trophy. We all wanted to be there to help him celebrate so we walked into the auditorium where they had all the trophies set up on a table on the stage. They were huge and beautiful! My God, they certainly didn't spare any expense for the league trophies. We had a great dinner and some drinks. I still didn't drink, other than the odd beer after a game. We all had our wives and girlfriends with us. I was dating a girl named Teresa at this point. A really pretty, but painfully shy girl who got embarrassed incredibly easy. She was a super nice person and way smarter than me. She became a pharmacist, got married, (not to me), and had some kids. When the time came to hand out the trophies, they gave out the best defenseman first. That went to a guy from Larry's. Most Sportsmanlike went to a guy from Larry's. Best Goalie, Larry's. When the Leading Scorer was awarded to Dave Watson, we all cheered, "Mad Dog, Mad Dog, Mad Dog!" Everyone who was awarded a trophy got a cheer from their own team and polite applause from everyone else. When the time came to give out the Most Valuable Player award, my girlfriend and I were hoping they would do it quickly so we could get out of there. She had to be home by midnight, because she was only 18, and it was already 11:30. Our coach, Gord, got to hand out the award, and we all gave him a huge round of applause. He said a few words about how successful the year was and that he hoped everyone would be back next season. "Now for the award of the night. The most valuable player in the North Shore Intermediate Recreational Hockey League for the 1981/82 season is… Jerry Hack!" You could've knocked me over with a feather. I had won MVP?! I couldn't believe it, "Are you shitting me?" was all I could think to myself. The whole room burst into applause. Every player from every team stood up and applauded. Apparently, I had a great season. I knew I had played well, but MVP? Inconceivable. What a way to end the year. I was on cloud 9. My girlfriend phoned home and told her mom what had happened, and she said Teresa could be home by 1:00 but no later.

So, we stayed and partied for an hour, and then I got her home for the appointed time. I took my trophy home and put it in my room. I showed it to nobody for the first while. I kind of wanted to keep it to myself, at least for the time being.

CHAPTER 9

The Merger

The 1982/83 season would start with some big changes. We didn't play summer hockey that year as not enough guys wanted to play. We rented the rink a couple of times in August just to get the rust off. When the season was about to start, I got a phone call from John Aitken. "The Kings are merging with another team," he told me. I wasn't sure what to think. Apparently, some of the guys were tired of losing and wanted to play elsewhere. Wade, Bruce, Earl, Frank (who would sing opera in the shower), Andy, Hugh, Hank and a few other guys were gone. Luckily, another team in the league was having the same problem, so we merged with The Golden Bears. John also informed me that the Burnaby Amateur Hockey League had folded. The 4 Rinks were starting their own league and had taken all their ice times away. I said to John that The Golden Bears were a pretty good team and that maybe we'll win more games this season. He didn't answer and cleared his throat and said that there was something else. The Golden Bears already had a goalie. John told me that the guy had played junior and was apparently some kind of superstar. I assumed the guy was like Lonnie in that he wanted to play all the games, and that I was out of luck. But John said that they wanted to go with two goalies, but that the other one was going to be Ron. Ron again. Was this guy ever going to make up his fuckin' mind? Well, I still had the Cottrell team to play for, and I was constantly getting phone calls to play for other teams, so I guessed there was not much I could do. Bummer. I was bummed because I wasn't going to get to play with John anymore, and I was going to miss the other guys too.

I was hanging around the next day waiting for the phone to ring when a call poured in. To my surprise, it was John again. Big news. The Golden Bears superstar goalie had decided not to play. He wanted to coach. So, a spot opened up, and I was in. Cool. What a difference a day makes. The season was rapidly approaching, and I couldn't wait. The summer had been long, and I was itching to play some games. Pickup hockey had become old hat for me. Competition was now my drug of choice. Playing just for fun wasn't really fun at all. That's probably a bad attitude, but it was the one I had at the time.

When all was said and done, there was me, John, Ron, Greg, and a couple of other guys from the Kings who joined The Golden Bears. Their roster included Greg Seeker, the captain, who reminded me of Ivan Boldirev, a defenseman named Larry (nicknamed "the human Zamboni," because he was always down on the ice collecting snow), another one named Marty, who was an absolutely fearless shot blocker. Ken Ludba, Craig Bolton, (who was like 9 feet tall on skates), James Blake, an absolute prince of a guy and someone who could always make you laugh. Dayne Knight, this guy would score a million points, and I never saw him break a sweat. Glenn Larssen, who was the fastest skater on the team and had a cannon of a shot. Then there was Scott Houston, who came over from The Colts. He was a playmaking centerman who could take over a game seemingly whenever he felt like it. And last, but not least there was the coach, Lance MacConnell.

The superstar goalie. He had played for the Vancouver Junior Canucks for a couple of years. He was a little shorter than me, but he had this air of confidence about him. One of those guys that liked himself and didn't feel the need to have to impress anyone. I was twenty-one when I met Lance, who was about five or six years older, and we took an instant liking to each other. He would be my goaltending mentor for the next few years. The fact that he had played junior impressed the hell out of me. I was in my third year of beer league hockey, and two years removed from falling backwards all the time.

One thing about the Golden Bears is we had the all-name team. If Hack was a bad name for a goalie, it was doubly bad for a golfer. Every time I tried to book a tee time at a course I had never played before, they would ask me my name. I would say "Hack", and they would say, "No really, what's your name?" One time I called up this course, and they asked me my name, and I said "Bond, James Bond." The guy wrote it in the book, no questions asked. Other guys on our team were named, Dan Hatch, Dayne Knight, Buster Burwash, and Tim Burr. Mr. Burr was like Snuffleupagus, because I never actually met the man. He was a forward and only played when I wasn't there.

Buster Burwash was no great shakes as a hockey player. He always seemed to be one step behind the play. But he was a world class harmonica player. I asked him to play, "If You Wanna Get to Heaven" by the Ozark Mountain Daredevils. It starts out with a country blues harmonica riff. Buster had about ten different harmonicas, and he picked out the one in the right key and he thought in his head for a couple of seconds, then played it flawlessly. I could swear I was listening to the band playing live.

James Blake, (not a member of the all name team, but I'm on a roll here), was a versatile player. He could play both forward and defense, but we used him on defense. This one game we were playing a team called the Marauders. James received a pass at the blue line and wound up for a slap shot. It took him so long to wind up that the Marauders goalie had time to come all the way from his crease to the blue line until he was directly in front of James. James took the shot and blasted it two feet right into the goalie's pads. James was so shocked that he did a "Shuffle Off to Buffalo" and fell down, smacking the back of his head on the ice. He was ok. James is a tough guy.

Dan Hatch was a big man, and he still is, I guess. He had these big lumbering strides, and the way he best helped the team was to stand in front of the other team's net. He was 6'3" and 235 lbs. He was like an eclipse to opposing goalies. Defensemen would try to move him out of there, but Dan was so strong it was a useless endeavor. There would end up being two guys screening the goalie instead of just one. Eventually, they just left him there.

Funniest thing about Dan was how he met his wife, Tina. Tina was a waitress in a nightclub. Dan took a shining to her, but there was never any time to start a conversation. Dan found out what car Tina drove, and then let the air out of one of the tires. He then showed up after her shift was over to help her fix it. They ended up getting married and have three beautiful daughters. I think Dan is lucky that the stalking laws weren't as stringent then as they are now.

That season we won more than we lost. I can't remember any of the other teams we played except for the Burnaby 4 Rinks Blues. They had Bernie and Jimmy Brown playing for them. The Brown brothers had played for the Kings the year before. They were really good hockey players. Bernie was the first player I ever saw who did the stickhandle-the-puck, drop-it-to-his-feet, and then kick-it-back-up, move. He used it all the time and scored quite a few goals that way. If I had to compare Jimmy to anyone, it would be Thoeren Fleury. He was a little guy, but feisty as hell. The problem with the Brown brothers was that they didn't have any money. Either that, or they were too cheap to pay for the season. They paid on a per game basis, and even then, it was hard getting money out of them. The rumour was they got to play for free on the 4 Rinks team.

When the season started, it was going to be me and Ron in goal. Just before the season began, Ron quit. He had something else going on in his life, and he just didn't have the time to commit to the team. I was going to miss him, he was a really good guy and a good goalie, but I wasn't going to miss him flip flopping between wanting to play out and play in goal. I was going to play every game now. I went from not having a team to now I was going to play every game. I couldn't help but think that there was some higher power at work. Maybe it was Randy.

As the season rolled along, I was making some great strides. Lance really knew his stuff. He never showed me anything on the ice. He just told me what he wanted me to do, and I tried to apply it to my game. He was always harping on me to play the puck, but I really sucked at it. I was naturally a right-handed shot, and I had my catching glove on my left hand. My natural inclination was to turn my stick around so that I could shoot right-handed, but Lance didn't want me to do that. He wanted me to learn to shoot left-handed. I was born left-handed. And there are actually a lot of things I can do with both hands. Like using hand tools, or eating with chopsticks, (I work for a Japanese company and it always freaks out the Japanese management when I show them this talent of mine), opening jars and bottles, etc. But shooting left-handed was nearly impossible for me. I couldn't even get the puck off the ice. I would flub it every time, and the puck would slide about ten feet. He kept on me all that season. I would keep working at it, but it seemed to be a useless endeavour. I just couldn't get it.

The other parts of my game were coming along fine. I was learning about angles, and rebound control, and following the play. After the games, Lance would critique me: poor, average, good, really good or great. I was getting a lot of goods, a few really goods, and even the odd great. After one game I had apparently played great, I came off the ice to the bench, and Lance was standing at the gate with this weird little smirk on his face. "I enjoy watching you play," is all he said. High praise indeed. Apparently, he was getting as much enjoyment in seeing me improve as I was in playing for him.

Lance taught me about keeping track of players. I learned how to know where everybody should be, and where everybody was. I could keep track of all ten players on the ice at any time. It came in handy when someone would try to sneak around behind me and get a backdoor pass. He also taught me how to talk to my defensemen. This was a problem because with my mask on, the players had a hard time understanding what I was saying. I sounded like Charlie Brown's teacher. Whah whah WHAH WHAH whah. This problem would be solved years later when I finally gave up the mask and switched to a helmet and cage.

That first year with The Golden Bears was a lot of fun. The only downside was that John had quit about halfway through the season. John was a good, solid defenseman. He had a knack of reading a play before it happened. He was especially good at 2 on 1's, and 3 on 1's. But the Bears had their defense set before the season began, so John had to play forward. Talk about square peg in a round hole. John just couldn't make the adjustment, and the frustration mounted. It came to a head when Lance played him for just one shift in a game. John didn't say a word. He just got changed, didn't even shower, and left. He didn't play another game for the Bears. He joined another team. I didn't see him as much, but we still hung out. After all, he was my big brother.

Chapter 10

Valhalla

The 1982/83 season ended with a loss, like almost all of them do. The 1983/84 season we changed leagues again. The Vancouver Amateur Hockey Association was a citywide league with about a hundred teams. It was set up like the English Premier soccer. The best teams were in Div. 1 and the worst teams were in Div. 12. Usually the top two teams in each division moved up and the bottom two teams moved down at the end of each season. Each team had a home ice time. Every week you played at the same time at the same rink. It was almost professional. I think we started in Div. 5, about halfway between the top and the bottom.

We had played a game at the 4 Rinks, the VAHA still had a couple of ice times there, and we all decided to make the short drive to the Villa Hotel for beers, instead of going up to the bar at the rink. It was an old fashioned "beer parlour" that had round tables with red stretchy cloth covers. We were all sitting around, shootin' the shit when I noticed this blonde girl sitting about 20 feet away. She was in the top ten most beautiful girls I had ever seen. What the hell was she doing in such a seedy bar? I couldn't stop looking at her. She was sitting there smoking a cigarette and drinking a girly drink. I just couldn't believe my eyes. She was a stunning blonde that just oozed sexiness. Some guy came up and spoke into her ear. I assumed it was her boyfriend. A girl like that HAD to have a boyfriend. I looked at the guy and thought what a fuckin' lucky guy, and then he stood up. It was Tye Fitzsimmons!! I was sure it was him. He looked exactly the same way he did when he played on Randy's team, just older, and he had a moustache. I figured he wouldn't remember me, so I didn't bother going over to talk to him. I just sat there, in awe of his girlfriend. As it turned out, one of the guys on the team knew Tye. They asked him if he was playing hockey at all. I could hear their conversation, and I heard Tye say that he was looking for a team to play for. We signed him up right then and there. Tye and I were going to be teammates. Randy strikes again.

Tye joined the team and became an instant sensation. He was a great player and played on a line with Dayne Knight and Glenn Larssen. Together they scored most of our goals, and we won a lot of games. Tye was a great player but he was an even better person. He was one of those guys who could talk to anybody about anything. He was always up for a party, and he always wanted to include everybody. He made sure that I was included in a lot of his plans. Another added bonus was that he was friends with Ian Frison, my childhood friend from Dominion Street. At one of our parties, I was talking to Ian, reminiscing about our childhood. We were standing next to an open door which led to the basement. Ian and I were talking when all of the sudden Ian throws himself down the basement stairs! He gets up and runs back up the stairs to where I was standing and continued what he was saying. I couldn't believe what I just saw. I asked him what the hell that was, and he just said it was something he liked to do, just to mess with people's heads. I went and found Tye and told him what had just happened, and he just chuckled and said that Ian did that all the time.

That season I was given my nickname. Over the first few seasons, guys tried to give me nicknames, but none of them stuck. Names like "Brick" for another brick in the wall, "Rebound", "I can't be rebound because all the shots go in," I would joke. The inevitable "Red Light," "Sieve," and "Swiss" for Swiss cheese. The one that stuck was given to me by Kelly Gladson. He had played junior with Lance and he was a hotshot. By far the best player on the team, just don't ask him to backcheck. He was an offensive player, and that was all he wanted to be. He was a funny guy and a real pistol. We had played an afternoon game, and I wasn't particularly sharp. We had lost something like 9-3. We were sitting in the dressing room doing what hockey players do, some getting changed, some drinking beer, some smoking, some smoking dope, some doing all of those things. I was just sitting there. I had taken off my chest protectors and arm pads, and I happened to look over at Kelly who was sitting directly across and staring at me. "You're a fuckin' teabag," he said, half serious, half joking. Everybody stopped talking and looked at him. Somebody asked, "Teabag? What is that supposed to mean?" I was even more perplexed. I didn't see the correlation between my play and a teabag. "Everything went through you," he said. The whole room exploded in laughter. "Hey Teabag!" someone yelled, and for the next five minutes all I heard was, "Teabag this", and Teabag that", "Teabag, Teabag, Teabag." From that point on, I was Teabag. Tye loved nicknames. He gave a lot of people their nicknames. "Mr. Pants", "Nobby", and quite a few others, but he fell in love with "Teabag." You can imagine, I wasn't exactly enthralled with this nickname, and I hoped it would die a quick death. It probably would have, but Tye wouldn't let it. One time I was playing for a team whose players only knew me as Jerry. The game was over, and I was getting changed, having my aftergame Pepsi, when guess who walks in, Tye. The guy seemingly knew everybody at 4 Rinks and was friends with one of the players on the team. He takes one look at me and says, "TEABAG!" One of the guys asks, "Teabag? Why Teabag?" Tye says, "Because everything goes through him!" Oh God, here we go again. "Teabag! What an awesome nickname. Hey Teabag!" Fuck. Whenever we would go to the bar or a party, Tye would call me from the other end, "Hey Teabag!" Someone would inevitably ask "Why Teabag?" And the whole process would repeat itself. After a few months, I caved and just accepted the nickname. I figured it could be a lot worse. I could be, "Red Light Lonnie."

It was also during this time that I got a job installing paving stones, the interlocking bricks that make driveways and patios and sidewalks. I was 22 when I started this job in the spring of 1984. The work was tough and grueling. A stack of bricks weighed 75 pounds, and you were back & forth all day carrying bricks from the pallet to wherever the guy who was laying them down. Sometimes I would have to go uphill, and other times downhill; all day, every day. That summer, I went from 155 pounds to 180 and my strength had improved dramatically. Before that summer, when I was playing hockey, if a guy was screening me, I would give him a shot in the middle of the back with my glove hand, and most of the time the guy would hardly move. The first time I played after that summer, a guy was standing in front of the net who was about the same size as me, and I gave him the standard shot in the back with the glove hand. I expected him to move just a little, but this time the guy's head whiplashed and he did a faceplant right on the ice. He got up and clocked me. I was in such shock I didn't even see it coming. I felt like Superman. The other good thing about the paving stone job was that over time if you were reliable and hard-working, you were upgraded to laying the stone. To do it properly, you had to stand with your legs straight and your feet about shoulder width apart, and are bent over at the waist. The stack of bricks would be centered and just a bit ahead of your feet. You would take the top brick in one hand and lay it down, while your other hand was grabbing the next brick, and you would lay that one down. Your arms had to act like pistons. If you let your upper body bounce up and down, your back wouldn't last long. I spent many days bent over, laying stone. Being in that position all day stretches your hamstrings. I became extremely flexible and after awhile, I could do the splits.

I will tell you just one story from my paving stone days. I was living with my girlfriend at the time, her name was Angela. She was 19 and I was 22. Her Mom absolutely hated the fact that we were living together. When Angie moved in with me, we went to her house to get her belongings. Her Mom was in the driveway, (which I had helped install, that was how we met), screaming at the top of her lungs directly at me, "God damn you Jerry! God damn you to hell! I wish you were DEAD!!" Her mom was a strange woman. She once purposely stepped on a slug with her bare foot just to gross me out. After the move, I wasn't welcome at Saturday dinners, as you can imagine. But that's not the story. We had an old Siamese cat named Sammy. Sammy was about 12 years old and had begun to lose his marbles. He began shitting behind the entertainment unit, where it was almost impossible to clean up. And it was not solid, not by a long shot and stunk to high heaven. We would have to move the whole entertainment unit forward. One of us would grab the cat and rub his nose in it, (not really in it, but you know what I mean). We took him to the vet, but she said that there was nothing physically wrong with him. So, we just put up with it. I was at work one day doing the cutting. Around the edges of the driveway or patio, there were always gaps that needed to be filled in. You had to take a full brick and cut it to the shape of the gap. We did this with a guillotine. It was a metal contraption that had two blades and worked like a jaw. You lifted the handle to raise the upper jaw, stuck the brick in and rested it on the lower jaw, lowered the handle so the upper jaw rested on top of the brick and then pushed the handle down the rest of the way. Usually the brick would just snap into two pieces. One piece would be the shape you needed to fill the gap. On this particular day, we got a substandard batch of bricks. They hadn't been stored long enough and were still quite soft. When you tried to snap them in two, they would just kind of mush down. I tried to cut this one brick, and a chunk came flying off and landed about 10 feet away. It was raining, and when I looked over at this chunk of brick, it looked exactly like a Sammy shit. I was wearing a hoodie with the big front pocket, so I went over and picked it up, put it in my pocket, and took it home with me. Later that night, Angie went in to the bathroom to brush her teeth before bed. I went and grabbed the piece of brick and went to the kitchen sink and got it wet. Then I went into the bedroom and placed it down on her side of the bed, just below her pillow. She finished in the bathroom, and did a couple of other things while I went into the bathroom to brush my teeth. She finally went into the bedroom. From our bathroom, if you wanted to see into the bedroom you had to peek around the corner. I did so, and could see Angie notice the brick. "Oh that fuckin' cat!" she said and stormed into the living room, grabbed Sammy and brought him into the bedroom, and rubbed his nose in it. She then took him into the living room and put him in his bed. "Bad bad kitty," she cursed at him. She came stomping into the bathroom where I was in the midst of trying to brush my teeth and not laugh. "We gotta get rid of that fuckin' cat!!"

she told me. I said nothing back. She rolled down some toilet paper, still cursing. "I can't believe he did that!" She brought the wad of toilet paper into the bedroom. I peeked around the corner again and saw her plug her nose and attempt to wipe it up. Of course, instead of needing to be wiped up, it came up in one big chunk. It took her a couple of seconds to realize what it was, but when she did, I got the blast. "Oh you fuckin' asshole!" she said as she came charging into the bathroom. I was in virtual hysterics as she yelled, "You made me punish the cat for nothing, you… ASSHOLE!" and she started smacking me across the arm. I said I was sorry, but I was laughing too hard and had a mouthful of toothpaste. She went to the cat and apologized and gave him some of his favourite treats. I went into the doghouse for the next two days. Sammy got treated like a king for a week solid. Angela and I broke up shortly thereafter.

Chapter 11

The Golden Years

The Golden Bears became a powerhouse. The 1983/84 year we won the Div.5 championship. It was my first, but I didn't even play in the final. I was on the bench and watched Dave Woodean play. He was my backup all year. He was a funny guy. During warm-up, he would yell at the players and tell them how horrible they were and how much they sucked. He was a pretty good goalie too. I learned a lot from Dave. Due to circumstances that occurred away from the rink at that time, my head just wasn't in the game. Lance decided to go with Woody, and it was the right decision. He was solid, and we won. Celebrating a championship that you didn't contribute to, is bittersweet. You're happy but a little empty.

That summer, for the second time, I got to play against a real live professional hockey player. Cliff Ronning had just been drafted by the St. Louis Blues and was the leading scorer in the Western Hockey League. He played for the New Westminster Bruins. I went down to the 4 Rinks to play casual hockey. Casual hockey is scheduled every day in the afternoon. Anybody can play, you just go to the rink and sign up. I usually couldn't make it to the rink during the day because I was working, but on this particular day, I got an unexpected day off, so I went to the rink. While I was signing up, I noticed Cliff's name on the list. I immediately got nervous. When I got to the dressing room, I didn't see him. He was in the other room. When I got out onto the ice, there he was. Holy shit. During the warmup, he shot on me a couple of times but took it easy. You could tell the guy was a pro. We split into teams, and Cliff was playing against me. As you might guess, he was by far the best player out there, and he wasn't even trying. He made me look stupid a couple of times. One time, he came in on me and made a deke, it was one I had seen a thousand times in the leagues I played in, so I just followed him to the side of the net and I was thinking, "I got you this time, I am fucking good!" Then he made a pass to someone else standing wide open in front of the net. I don't know how he even saw that guy, because I hadn't. When you play beer league hockey, sometimes you can start thinking that you are better than you are. Whenever you play against someone of this caliber, it really does a job on you. It makes you realize just how really far away you are from the dream. Cliff went on to play more than a thousand games in the NHL and was the best player I ever played against, even if it was just that one time.

Just as a side story, John played casual hockey one afternoon with a friend of his. They decided to go up to the bar and have a quick beer before heading home. Since they weren't going to be long they just left their sticks and equipment bags at the bottom of the stairs that led into the bar. When they emerged a little later John noticed that someone had stolen his hockey stick. His friend advised him to check the rinks and see if someone was using it. So they went to the rinks where games were going on. Sure enough, one of the players had John's stick. John waited until the guy got close enough, opened the gate and ran out onto the ice and tackled him. He then retrieved his stick and walked out of the rink. Surprisingly, nobody challenged John, they just let him leave.

The 1984/85 season ended the same way as the previous season, with two notable exceptions. We won the Div. 4 championship, and I played all the playoff games. The exhilaration of playing on a championship winning team was everything I had hoped it would be. If there's a word for joy times a thousand, that would be the word to describe how I felt. I didn't play in the summer after that season. I was playing about 100 games a season (my record was 111). I was playing pretty much every time anyone asked me to. I loved playing games, but pickup hockey was a drag. I needed that competition to get my adrenaline pumping. If I needed to practice something, I figured that during a game was the best time. The Cottrell team folded after having been knocked out of the playoffs early that season, but I was always getting phone calls from teams asking me to play full time. Basically, I would have my pick. I would play full time for two teams and spare for a bunch more. The Golden Bears were my main team and took precedence over any other.

In the 1985/86 season, The Bears finished second in Div. 3 and got moved up to Div. 2 for the 1986/87 season. The difference between divisions is usually one or two players. Moving up from Div. 5 to Div. 4 to Div. 3, we didn't really add anybody. Our good players, Kelly, Tye, Dayne, and Glenn carried us. I was getting better all the time as well. That's what happens when you play against good players, you improve. But as you go up, the goalies get better, and good teams have no weak players. I can't say that we didn't have any weak players. We had a few and a lot of average players. They were exposed against Div. 2 teams. The difference between Div. 2 and Div. 3 was night and day, and we struggled. Most teams would just puck control us to death. We won a few games, but it was a lost cause. A couple of months into the season, we were demoted back to Div. 3.

CHAPTER 12

Game Changer

The 1986/87 season was moving towards Christmas. The Bears had been demoted to Div. 3 and were cruising along with around a .500 record. Div. 3 had gotten a lot better since we left and we were having trouble winning games. It was around November 20th that I was at home reading, "The Province" newspaper on a rare night off from playing. I was reading the sports section checking up on my Vancouver Canucks. They were again in last place of the Smythe division. I turned the page and noticed an ad at the bottom of the page. It read, "Senior Hockey Team in Saskatchewan looking for two forwards and a goalie." I kind of thought that it would be cool to play in Saskatchewan. My father was born in Shaunavon, and we still had relatives there. It was just a fleeting thought, and I kept turning the pages. After a few minutes, I figured I would look at the ad again. "Senior Hockey Team in Saskatchewan looking for two forwards and a goalie." Underneath that, it had a phone number, and underneath that, it said, "Salary negotiable." I started thinking to myself that there wasn't anything really keeping me from going. My job was seasonal, and if I wanted the winter off, I'm sure I could get it. I didn't know anything about Senior hockey in Saskatchewan, but I had seen the Burnaby Lakers play a few times with Randy and John. The Lakers were a senior team that had played against the Kimberly Dynamiters and the Trail Smoke Eaters back in the day. I figured I would give it a shot. All they can do is say no.

I phoned the phone number listed in the paper, and a woman answered. I told her I was phoning about the ad in the Vancouver Province newspaper. She said that she would get her husband. I heard her tell "Howard" that the phone was for him. He got on the phone and said, "Howard Mehain, Hello." I told him I had read the ad in the Vancouver Province and that I might be interested in coming for a tryout. He asked me about my playing experience. I made the mistake of telling him the truth. I told him that I was a goalie and had started playing when I was 18, and that I had only played recreational beer league hockey. But that I was really pretty good and a lot of the guys had told me I was the best goalie they ever played with. This last part was a lie, a couple of guys had said that to me but none of the really good players. The good ones all considered Lance to be the best goalie they ever played with. Howard said, "Uh-huh", he paused for a second and continued "Well that sounds great! We haven't decided on who we're going to bring out here, but I will write down your information and give you a call when we make a decision." I thanked him, and we said goodbye. It was a total brushoff. I could tell that he hadn't written down my info, but at least he had left the door open a crack. He didn't say no. It was a Wednesday night, and I figured I would give him a couple of days, and I would call him back. When Friday night came, I called him back. His wife answered again and she handed the phone to Howard. I re-introduced myself and asked if they had made any decisions yet. He told me that they had put that ad in all the papers in Western Canada and were still seeing what kind of interest it would stir up. He said he had my name and number and would call in a week or so if anything transpired. I knew he was just giving me the brushoff again and wouldn't call. I figured I would give him another few days and call him again. He was either going to give me a tryout or tell me to go fuck myself. In any case, I wasn't going to let it go. Another few days passed, and I phoned again. I really hated being incessant, it goes against my nature, but something inside me said that this opportunity was not going to present itself again. This time his wife answered and said that Howard wasn't home. There was kind of an awkward silence, and she said that Howard was the General Manager for the team, but Frank Hamel was the President, and that maybe I should give him a call. I got the feeling that Howard had probably told her about this beer league goalie who kept bugging him for a tryout, but I was happy to talk to anybody. I wrote down the number, and I phoned Frank Hamel. He picked up the phone. I told him that I had spoken to Howard a couple of times and gave him the same story that I had given to Howard. I got the same, "Uh-huh" that I got from Howard, but then he said, "Well, we're not going to turn anyone away, if you want to pay your way out here, we'll give you a shot." I tried to stay calm. "Salary negotiable," kept running through my head. John and I had always talked about how great it would be to get paid to play hockey. Neither one of us could imagine what that would be like, and I was going to get a chance to do just that. I thanked Frank and told him I would be in touch after I had made the arrangements. We said our goodbyes, and I hung up the phone. I slammed my hand down on the table and gave a loud WOO-HOO!

I thought about everything I would have to do. I would have to rent storage space for my furniture. Give notice on my apartment. Tell my boss I would need at least a couple of weeks off, if not the rest of the winter. I would need to arrange for somebody to cover my games with the Bears. I called a goalie that I played against. He was a friend-of-a-friend-of-mine, and we had actually hung out a few times, the three of us. His team had two goalies, and I asked him if he and the other guy would cover my games until I got back. He was excited for me and said that they would cover the games, no problem. I would need winter clothes. I had heard it gets to like... -500°C in Saskatchewan. I didn't even know where I was going. I hadn't bothered asking what town they were in. I got busy. I went to work the next day. I had told the boss previously that the possibility existed that I could get a tryout out of town, and I might need a couple of weeks off, maybe even the rest of the winter. When I told him that I was actually going, he wished me well and made sure that I had my separation slip so that I could apply for unemployment benefits. I rented a storage space and paid for a month. I didn't know if I would be on the next plane back or what. I gave a month's notice on my apartment and got it all cleaned up. I bought some winter clothes and boots. I checked out plane fares, but it was too expensive to fly. I would have to buy a one-way ticket, and worst-case scenario, if I didn't make the team, (of which there was a high likelihood), I would have to buy a one-way ticket back. I decided to take the train. The bus would be faster, but it would also be more cramped. Also, the bus allowed smoking, on the train you could ask for a non-smoking car. I bought my train ticket, and I was set. I stayed at my sister's house for a couple of days waiting for my train to leave. I spoke to Howard to tell him when I was going to be there. I even found out the name of the town. Assiniboia. I had heard of the Assiniboine river in Manitoba, but Howard informed me that they were two separate things. Assiniboia was about 100 km's south of Moose Jaw. Howard sounded kind of pissed that I was even coming. I guess he figured I was just some beer league loser, who had no chance of playing for his team and that this was a total waste of time and money. I guess I couldn't blame him. In his shoes, I would've thought the same thing.

"So, with my faithful dog, Shithead, leading the way," (sorry, I just love that movie. No, I did not have a dog with me) I got on the train at Maple Ridge. My sister dropped me off. I had with me enough clothes to last three months. They were all jammed into one carry-on bag. I was surprised that the zipper didn't break. It was chock full and bursting at the seams. I had my hockey bag, (also stuffed) and two sticks. It was a nice winter day in the Lower Mainland. It was sunny and probably 10°C. There was no room anywhere for the winter boots I had bought, so I had to wear them. I'm sure I looked pretty foolish, but I really didn't care what other people thought of me. There were two girls about my age that were getting on at the same stop as me. My impression of them was, "bar chicks." Another girl was dropping them off, and they were all laughing and joking around. I'm a pretty shy guy, so I didn't say anything and just waited for the train. When it finally arrived, they went to the car on the left, the smoking car, and I was in the car on the right. I saw them a few times on the trip, in the dining car, and when they would walk through my car to go to the sightseeing car. But I never did speak to them. In my car was one other guy, and he immediately laid down and went to sleep. It was going to be a good trip if it was just the two of us.

The trip was going to take 31 hours. The other guy in the car seemed to sleep the whole time. He only seemed to wake up to go to the bathroom. I don't remember him eating anything the whole time. In Calgary, this girl got on and sat across the aisle from me. She was blonde, pretty, about 2 or 3 years younger than me if I had to guess. Like I said before, I'm a pretty shy guy and initiating a conversation with a member of the opposite sex does not come naturally to me. But after some time, I got up enough nerve to ask her where she was going. She said Regina. I told her I was going to Moose Jaw. We ended up talking the whole way to Moose Jaw. She was very intelligent and friendly. I liked her right away. I don't remember her name. When the train arrived, we parted ways. She gave me her phone number. Over the next couple of weeks, we talked on the phone a couple of times but whatever connection we felt on the train just fizzled and died. I never saw her again, but she did make the trip go faster.

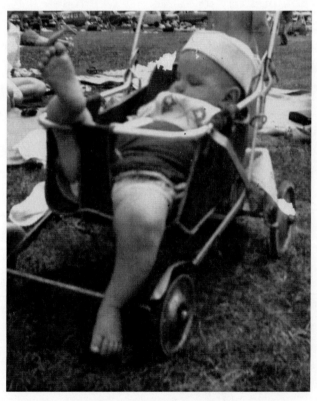

The earliest known picture of me.
In my dream I am probably making a kick save.

My best friend Randy Aitken, who tragically passed away at the age of 16 from cancer. His death would shape my attitude of how I was going to live the rest of my life.

Randy's last team photo. He's in the middle row, second from the right. He didn't play at all that season and he was just a few months from passing away when this photo was taken. You can tell he is the only one not wearing his equipment. He was in his street clothes and just put the jersey on for the picture. Tye Fitzsimmons is in the same row. He's the blonde kid wearing an "A" on his jersey. Rick Egerton is the goalie in front of Randy. It was his family who paid to take Randy to Hawaii, knowing that he was terminally ill.

Me in 1983. The trophy on the left is for having the Best Goals Against Average in the entire V.A.H.A (Approximately 100 teams. Dave Woodean and I combined for a 3.05 G.A.A.) The trophy on the right is for M.V.P. in the North Shore Intermediate Recreational Hockey League. If you look closely, mine is the only name engraved along the bottom. I was supposed to give the trophy back, but no one ever asked for it, so I kept it. Dave "Mad Dog" Watson kept his scoring champion trophy as well.

Me playing in Fairbanks, Alaska. I believe this was the game we won and I stopped over fifty shots. I couldn't stop looking at the girl in the white dress in the top left of the photo.

Accepting the trophy for "Player of the Game" from Garth Hordenchuk. The team we played was a junior team from Minnesota, The St. Paul Vulcans.

We were always partying. Here is Gary Peck (in the Hugo Boss shirt). Scotty Wray is mugging for the camera. While he was playing for Moose Jaw, I once punched Scotty in the nose hard enough to stagger him back a couple of steps. I always expected payback but it never came. Cliff Mapes has his back to the camera.

Brent Castle and I had a song that we would sing after every victory.

Game 2 of the Provincial Finals in Eston against The Ramblers, 1990. There was no barrier to keep the fans separated from the players. On the other side of the arena were the bleachers. The first row of fans sat with their feet on top of the boards. A couple of our players were spat on. We lost this game 7-4 and had to drive all that night to get to Tisdale for Game 2 of the league final.

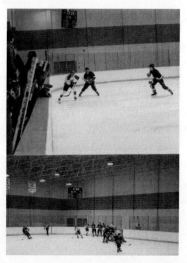

The league championship game in Tisdale, 1990. In the above photo you can see we are down 7-4 with 17 minutes to go. In the lower photo you can see with less than 4 minutes to go we are ahead 9-7. We would score one more to win 10-7. We scored 5 goals in a span of about 3 ½ minutes right after the P.A. announcer announced that Game 3 would be played the next afternoon.

Howard Mehain holding the League Championship Trophy with coach Art Birss looking on. We couldn't drink out of a trophy, so we taped a beer glass to it so we could celebrate properly. You can see Scott Binner on the left. His T-Shirt got soaked and torn in the jubilation.

My girlfriend Terrie and I on the bus ride home after winning the league championship.

Warming up for the Provincial Championship game.
That's Scott Binner warming me up.
There were over 1,400 fans jammed into an arena that seats 914.

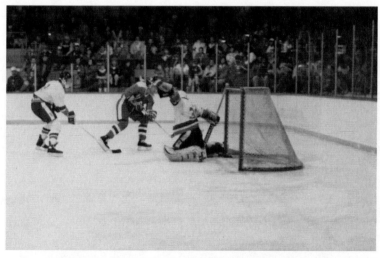

Making a save during the Championship Game.
It was so loud that you couldn't hear the whistle.

Celebrating with The Henderson Cup. Jim Misener
(who always had a better moustache than me) is refilling it for me.

Mike Bloski sitting on my lap after winning the Provincial title. He was happier for me than I was for myself. Brent Castle is helping us celebrate with The Henderson Cup. Brent had gone to 10 provincial finals in various sports and had lost them all. Not this time.

Me and Coach Art Birss holding each other up. Art was the only coach who truly believed in me, (honourable mention to Kim Waiting) and was always in my corner. We celebrated long into the night after winning the Provincial Championship.

The entire Rebel team after winning our second Provincial Title. The team executive as well as all the midget players who played with us are in this photo. I didn't know it at the time, but this was my last game in a Rebel uniform.

One of the few pictures of me playing in a Whitehorse Husky uniform.
That's Tommy "2 goals" Dobos entering the frame.

The famed DC-3 which we flew on to get from
Whitehorse to Fairbanks and Anchorage.

The 1991/92 Whitehorse Huskies. Next to me is Dennis Salamandyk.
To this day, the best goalie I ever played with or against.

The Russian team we played. Note the player on the bottom left. Somebody
from our team gave him a pair of our gloves because his were in such poor
shape. With the Soviet Union breaking apart, money was tight and their
equipment was something to be desired, to say the least.

Star Photo by MIKE THOMA:

HACK STOP — Nannock Warriors' goaltender Jerry Hack made this spectacular save er route to Nannock's 4-2 win versus Inuvik Huskies in Saturday action from the Yukon Indiar Hockey Association's tournament in Whitehorse over the weekend. Nannock lost a 5-3 heartbreaker to Lower Post in the 'A' division final.

A picture that appeared on the front page of the Whitehorse newspaper.

CHAPTER 13

Destiny

When I arrived, the team had just played a game in Moose Jaw against the powerhouse Moose Jaw Generals. The Generals had won the Hardy Cup in 1985. The Hardy Cup was symbolic of the Senior AA Canadian Hockey Championship, and the Generals were perennial challengers for this trophy. Howard Mehain met me as I got off the train, along with two of the players, Kevin Silzer and Chris Dumont. Kevin was a defenseman, and Chris was one of the goalies. They probably were thinking I was one of those tourists who dressed for the arctic tundra. I had worked security at Vancouver International Airport and had seen American tourists come off the plane in June wearing winter jackets and boots. Kevin, Howard and Chris were dressed in light jackets with t-shirts underneath, and jeans with running shoes. I was dressed in a heavy winter coat, sweat pants and snow boots. They didn't say anything about how I was dressed, but they must've been laughing inside. Chris grabbed my hockey bag, and Kevin grabbed my, bursting at the seams, carryall bag, leaving me with only my two goalie sticks. It was a short walk to the bus. The weather was maybe -10°C, and there wasn't any snow on the ground. I kind of laughed at myself for not checking the weather conditions before leaving Vancouver. On the walk to the bus, Howard gave me an update on the team. The Assiniboia Southern Rebels had just been beaten by the Generals 14-2. They had scored the first two goals and given up fourteen-straight. The team's record was now 0 wins and 10 losses. They had given up over 100 goals and scored 15. I was beginning to wonder what I had gotten myself into. I also wondered why Howard was happy to see me. He had been a bit of a jerk on the phone. I'm guessing he was hoping that any change might be a change for the better. He told me that the ad they had run in the newspapers all over Western Canada had resulted in some new players coming into town over the next little while, and he was hoping that the team's fortunes would change. We would see. I got on the bus and was introduced to the coach, Kim Waiting, and to some of the players. There were about 10 guys on the bus who played for the team. The others had gone home in their own transportation back to Regina, or whatever town they were living in. Not all the players lived in Assiniboia. Andy was the bus driver. He was nice, if not that talkative. I shook his hand. Half the guys were in the back playing the inevitable card game, and the others, including Kevin and Chris, were in the front. On the trip to Assiniboia, we talked hockey mostly. Kim told me that he had played against Brian Trottier when he was younger. I re-stated my hockey experience leaving out the statement of the guys who said I was the best goalie that they ever played with. Kim said, "Uh-huh." I'm sure they were all less than impressed with my resume, but they were really good guys. You could tell. I don't remember who else was on the bus in that initial bus ride. I'm sure some of the guys who would play the rest of that first season were there, but I was a stranger in a strange land, and I was a bit overwhelmed to tell you the truth. And nobody mentioned the accident.

When the bus arrived in Assiniboia, it went straight to the rink. Everybody disembarked and went to their cars. Howard gave me and Chris a ride. We drove to one of the three hotels in town. Howard got me registered and paid for a three-night stay. I asked Chris if he wanted to meet for lunch the next day, and he said yes, and then said no, that we could do dinner instead. I figured okay, dinner it is and expected him to show up around five or six in the evening. They left, and I went to my room for the night. I couldn't sleep. There wasn't a T.V. in the room, so I just laid there soaking in everything I had seen and heard so far and fell asleep about an hour later.

I arrived in Assiniboia Dec. 2nd, 1987. It was a Wednesday. The day before that, there was a horrible car accident just outside of town. When you drive into Assiniboia from the east, the highway has an "S" curve and there is an access road that leads into town just at the start of the "S." However, about 100 yards before that, there is an entry point to a farmers field that goes over a ditch. Underneath the entry point is a culvert, so the water can continue running and not overflow the banks and flood the field. It looks deceivingly like the access road entry to town. Even people who have lived there all their lives have to do a double take and remember to keep going, or they'll end up in the farmers field. Five teenage friends were returning from a rehearsal for a concert or play or something and were driving back into town. A witness who passed them going the other way said they were all jammed into the cab of a pickup truck. I am paraphrasing, but he said that they were going like a bat out of hell. Apparently, they were fooled by the entry into the farmer's field and drove right over top of the culvert. The pickup truck bounced downwards when it went off the road, and the culvert ripped into the gas tank. The pickup truck burst into flames. All five died instantly.

R.I.P

Carey Jay Shenher, 17
Trent Johnson, 17
Gary Leaver, 19
Mark Smith, 17
Robert Kimball, 16

Assiniboia at that time had a population of about 2,000 people, and if you included the surrounding towns, it swelled to maybe 3,000 or so. After the accident, the whole town was in mourning. The mood was somber, and you could feel it. It was palpable. My arrival in town could not have come at a worse time.

When I woke up that Wednesday morning, it was probably around 9:00. I got up, showered and went for breakfast in the hotel restaurant. The team covered my stay, but I had to pay for my food. No problem. I bought a couple of magazines at a store close by. I wasn't worried about getting lost. The town just wasn't big enough for that. There was Main Street, which was about 4 blocks long, the highway intersected Main Street at the north end. Most of the businesses in town were on these two streets. As soon as you left Main Street, it was all residences. The houses looked mostly like they were 20 or 30 years old at least, with the odd modern house mixed in. I settled back in my room with my magazines and was hoping that someone would come by to show me around, since Chris wasn't going to be there until at least 5 o'clock. At exactly noon, there was a knock on the door. I opened it, and there was Chris. He asked if I was ready for dinner. It took me about 3 seconds to realize that in Saskatchewan, it was breakfast, dinner, supper. Not breakfast, lunch, dinner like in Vancouver. I was still full from breakfast, but what the hell? I figured I could eat some more. We went to the Bar-B, a restaurant/bar/motel which sponsored the team. The whole town was in shock about the accident, but I hadn't heard about it yet. Chris didn't tell me, and we just made small talk while we had our dinner, I mean lunch? He was a local whose parents farmed outside of town. He didn't seem to view me as his competition. He was friendly and accommodating. We finished our meal, and he drove us to the sporting goods store. Frank Hamel, the president of the Rebels, and the man who had invited me for the tryout, was the owner of the "Recreation Sportshop." He was on the phone to somebody from the Weyburn Devils, another team in our league. The Devils were the next opponent for the Rebels and were supposed to play this coming weekend. Frank was explaining the situation to whoever was on the other end, and they were agreeing to postpone the game to a later date. He hung up the phone, and Chris introduced us. Frank was very friendly and seemed like a great guy. So far, everyone I had met seemed the same way. He brought me into his office and explained to me about the accident. It now made sense why everyone was walking around in such a massive daze. We finished talking about it and got down to the subject at hand. My tryout. He said that Howard was really hoping to sign someone with professional experience, or at least major junior experience. Someone who had at least played in the Western Hockey League. Turns out, the ad they had placed had resulted in a lot of players answering, but few goalies and nobody with the experience that they were seeking. They had just basically given me a tryout because I was so insistent, and nobody else was applying for the job. That was fine with me. I had no idea what I was getting into. I just had, "salary negotiable," stenciled on my brain. He told me the deal. I would get one practice on Friday night. If I showed enough ability in that one practice, I would get one game. If I showed enough ability in that one game, I would be signed for the rest of the season. If not, I was on the next train home. I thought that was fair enough. Even if I didn't like the deal, what was I going to do? It's not like I had a lot of leverage. I was a hockey nobody. I waited for the practice on Friday.

CHAPTER 14

Trial by Fire

Friday came, and it was time to go to the rink. I got there about an hour early, and I was given the stall right next to the door that leads to the ice. The dressing room was quite nice. When you walked in, the whole floor was carpeted. The coach's office was immediately to the right, and to the left were the showers. Straight ahead was the main dressing room with a lot of hooks underneath shelves that lined the walls up above straight wooden benches on three sides of the room. There was enough space to fit about twenty players comfortably. Across from me and to my left was the stick room. Everyone who played for the team were given free sticks and tape. As well as free skate sharpening. Cool. That would be nice not to have to pay for sticks.

The player in the stall next to me was introduced to me by Kim Waiting as "History." Nothing else, just "History." He was about 5' 7" tall and maybe 150 pounds. I never asked him his name, and he never offered it. I told him he must be pretty fuckin' good if everyone called him, "History." He just nodded his head and said that, "Yeah, I'm probably the best player here." I guessed that he was pretty fuckin' good. Nobody else really introduced themselves. I guess being the new guy, I was going to have to prove myself before getting to know anyone. Chris was there, and Kevin too, everyone seemed to be familiar with each other and were doing the locker room banter thing. I had to wear a helmet and cage, the mask that Vic made for me was not CSA approved and therefore illegal in the eyes of Senior Hockey Leagues. Not a big deal, I had a helmet and cage that I liked. The cage was a "cat's eye" mask, (the vast majority of NHL goalies use a "cat's eye" mask. If you have no idea what I'm talking about, you can Google it), and I had used it in games back home.

I got dressed and went on the ice. The arena was fairly small by Vancouver standards. It was basically a barn with a hockey rink inside of it. The ice cleaning machine wasn't even that. It was a farm tractor with an ice cleaning attachment on the back of it. The stands were all on one side of the rink and then wrapped around one end. There was a small booth for radio play by play. I was told that the rink sat 914 people. There was a score clock at the far end, opposite the stands. The lighting was good, one thing I hated was bad lighting in a hockey rink. I skated around a bit and did my stretches. I let Chris choose his net first. I didn't want to step on any toes. He chose the net at the far end, so I took the net at the near end. To my right, in the stands, there stood a dozen or so men. They were all staring at me. I felt like a fish in a fish tank. I noticed that Frank and Howard were among them. I took my warmup shots, trying to make sure I controlled all my rebounds. The low shots to the corners and shots to my body either stuck to me, or dropped to my feet, and I swept them into the corner. Most of the guys had really hard shots. In beer league, usually only one or two guys could really shoot the puck. Here, it was almost everyone. Everyone, except History. His shots were average at best, and that's being generous. I felt good. It was a cold day, and the heaters weren't on so I felt wide awake. I was doing fairly well so far. Nobody made me look stupid yet.

Kim Waiting blew the whistle, and we did some skating drills. Nothing that I couldn't do. I wasn't nervous. I was excited. Even though this could be my one and only opportunity, I was feeling confident. Now the shooting drills started. The guys lined up in three lines and one by one they skated in and took shots on me, alternating lines. First from my right, then straight at me, then from my left. I was letting in the odd goal but only on good shots. Then the St. Louis drill. Everybody went to either corner, one guy skates to the blue line, circles back and takes a pass from someone in the opposite corner. He comes in on goal and takes a shot, then the guy who passed the puck, circles around and takes a pass, and so on and so forth. Everything's good so far. Then we get into line rushes. Now it was time to shine, I thought. All the forwards separated in threes and the defenseman separated into pairs. Kim blew the whistle and 3 forwards took off and skated toward the net. A pair of defensemen tried to stop them. It was pretty fast. I could tell most of these guys had played some high-level hockey. All except History. Like I said, he was average at best. He was definitely not the same caliber as everyone else. He was a little slower than everyone. Everything about the guy was average. The best thing he could do was stop. He stopped really well. We did line rushes for a little while and then a few more drills, and then a fifteen-minute scrimmage. I felt I had held my own. It didn't seem to be anything I couldn't handle. I was hoping I had passed the initial phase of the audition. When we all got back into the dressing room, I asked Kevin how he thought I did. "Pretty good," he said. I got undressed and headed into the shower. After I dried off and got dressed, Kim called me into his office. The first moment of truth. He asked me how I thought I did, I said I thought I was okay, maybe even pretty good. He said that they had a game coming up on Sunday in

Gravelbourg against the Hornets. I just stood there. "You're starting," he said. I hadn't realized I was holding my breath. I let out a huge sigh. Kim laughed. He asked me if I had any questions. I asked where Gravelbourg was. He said it was a town about the same size as Assiniboia, and it was 45 minutes away by bus. I asked if they had a good team. He said they did. They had a very fast team and probably the best goalie in the league. I kind of hesitated and told him I had one last question. I stated that the guy they called "History" didn't seem to be all that great, why did they call him that. Kim smiled and said, "Because as soon as we have enough players, he's history." We both had a laugh, and as I was leaving Kim's office, I thought to myself that the hockey world can be cruel. Funny as hell, but cruel at the same time. I was almost afraid to tell him that my nickname was "Teabag."

Friday morning Howard came to my hotel and paid up until Monday morning. I was going to spend at least the next three days in this little town. I met a few people. On Saturday morning after breakfast, there was a knock on my door. I answered it and this guy was standing there. He was one of the dozen guys who were standing at the glass, watching me during practice the night before. I recognized the San Francisco 49ers jacket. He introduced himself as Bill Adamack, and he was on the Rebels team executive board. All the men who were watching me were on the executive board. He figured I might be bored and asked if I wanted to come out to his farm and hang out for awhile. I said sure. I grabbed my jacket and my big winter boots, and we went outside of town to his farm. We talked about all sorts of things. Mostly about the Rebels. He told me that this was their second season and that they were wanting to start a successful program and hoping that players would want to come from all over to play for them. He told me that they were looking forward to seeing me play on Sunday. I told him I wasn't quite sure what I was getting into, but I hoped that they would sign me after Sunday's game. We spent a few hours at his farm feeding the animals, and taking some grain to the grain elevator. He collected a cheque for $1,500. I thought it was cool that whenever he needed money, he would just cash in some grain. After that he then drove me back to my temporary home. The hotel I was staying at was never full during winter, so they opened up a room and set up a tv so I could have something to do. I did other things to kill time as well. I went to the rink and watched the Bantams practice. The goalie was pretty good. I went up and down Main Street and looked in all the stores. Chris came by a couple of times, and we would hang out. He was only 19. I thought he was older, 23 or 24. He had played minor hockey in Assiniboia growing up. He was a really nice kid. Some more players were arriving in town and were going to play on Sunday. A trial by fire, so to speak. Saturday was much the same as Friday. As the game drew closer, I really didn't feel nervous at all. It was like I was supposed to be there, and that this was the first step in a long journey.

Sunday finally came. I got a good night's sleep and had breakfast around 8:00. The game was at 1:00 in the afternoon. I had always preferred to play at night, but what was I going to do? It's not like they were going to change the game time because of me. I headed to the rink around 10:30. The bus was to leave at 11:00. We all met in the dressing room, coaches and players. I met the other goalie. His name was Bingo. He was a first nations guy, very friendly and easy to talk to. He started telling me about the league and other teams. He said he also played for Cupar, which was north of Regina. They were in a different league than us. He offered to fix my pads. He noticed that there was a hole in one of them. He had taught himself how to do leatherwork. I said I might take him up on that. We got on the bus, and I sat somewhere in the middle. I didn't want to sit up front with the coaches, and I didn't want to sit at the back with the veterans who immediately started playing cards. I took a window seat. The butterflies were starting to flutter but not too badly. I was looking out the window lost in thought when Darren Lucier sat beside me. He introduced himself and then started talking. He was from Hudson Bay, and he was a defenseman and captain of the team. He said he had played all over the province growing up. He also was first nations. He said he was related to Louis Riel, and then he made a stupid joke. I thought that was awesome. Darren would become my first friend on the team. We got along really well.

We arrived at the rink and everyone grabbed their equipment. I went to my stall and started to put on my stuff. When I put on my skates, they were like -1000 degrees kelvin. A couple of the guys laughed at me and said I had better learn to bring my skates onto the bus with me. I hadn't even noticed that everyone else had brought their skates on board. That was lesson #1. I used a blow dryer to heat them up and then got dressed. We took to the ice for the warmup. I still wasn't that nervous. Just excited. I was used to a five-minute warmup in beer league hockey, but in senior hockey it's twenty minutes. Bingo was the other goalie for this game, I went in took my shots, then he went in. We alternated the entire time, half and half. Then we went back to the dressing room. Weird. They did an ice clean before the game. I definitely wasn't used to that. While the ice was being cleaned, the coach got called out into the hallway. He came back and told me I couldn't wear my "cat's eye" mask. That they weren't CSA approved. Apparently, the goalie on the other team had pointed it out to the referees. Great. Bingo said his was ok, and that I could use it. I tried it on, got it adjusted, and we were good to go. Only problem was, there was a bar on the cage that was right in my line of vision. The only way I could see through it was to tuck my chin in as far as it would go and look through the gaps at the top of the cage, just under the helmet line. I had no choice. It was sink or swim time.

We went onto the ice to start the game and HOLY SHIT! there's people in the stands! I was used to playing in front of friends and family. There were about two hundred and fifty people sitting there! They must have come in when the ice was being cleaned, because there weren't more than twenty people there before. The butterflies just started doing double time. They played "Oh Canada" before the game started. We all had to line up on the blue line. Something else I had never experienced before. When that was over, the team congregated at the net. Only the starting five were allowed on the ice to prevent brawls from breaking out. I tried not to look in the stands, but man, that was distracting. All those people paid money to watch me play. It felt surreal. The game started, and Wow! It was way faster than I had expected. I was in way over my head, I felt like I was playing in a blender. With all the new players on our team, you had to expect that some adjustments would need to be made. Guys weren't used to playing with each other, or with me. The other thing that was a big distraction was that it was full contact. Up to this point, I had played exactly one game where hitting was allowed. I wasn't used to guys trying to bodycheck each other. My head was spinning, I felt like Linda Blair in "The Exorcist". About three minutes in, I had made a couple of easy saves. My defensemen seemed to really know what they were doing. They kept the shots to the outside. Then, someone dumped the puck in about 4 feet wide of the net. I went to play the puck and shoot it around the net, but I couldn't see the puck with Bingo's cage on. I totally flubbed it, and one of the Hornet players skated in from the other side of the net, pulled the puck in front and put it in the net before I could get back there. Shit. Nice start dimwit. I decided playing the puck was out. I would just stay in the net and stop the goddamn thing. And that I did. I made some really good saves, maybe even a couple of great ones. But I was also getting lucky. One of the Hornet forwards got around our defenseman to my right, he had a clear path to the net. He made a bit of a deke, and I went for it, he then pulled the puck to his backhand, I just kind of flopped to my left, paddy stacker style, he tried to tuck it underneath me, which was the right thing to do. He would've scored but the puck hit the knob of my stick behind me. One of my defensemen got back in time to see the puck laying there and pushed it back underneath me. I just laid on it until the referee blew the whistle.

The game went on like that. I made some saves, and some shots that I didn't see just hit me. We got down 2-0 in the second period, and I didn't think we were going to score, ever. The other goalie was amazing. He was really smooth. You could tell he had some really good coaching. Technically, he just didn't make any mistakes. If we were going to score on him, it was going to have to be a great play. He was left-handed, which means his catching hand was his right hand. A mirror image of me. His glove hand was very good, but it was his blocker hand that impressed me the most. You could not beat him blocker side. His name was Darren Komonoski. His cousin Ward had played goal for the Prince Albert Raiders and was the MVP of the Memorial Cup in 1985. Darren had played some junior as well, I think he said in Swift Current, but don't quote me on that.

The game stayed 2-0 for the longest time. Late in the 2nd period, we finally got one past their goalie. 2-1. The 3rd period starts, and the Rebels were starting to gel. The new players were making the adjustments, and I was keeping them in the game. With about 10 minutes remaining, they got another goal. The Hornets had this one line that was made up of three brothers. The Gaucher's (pronounced GOshay). All three were like whirling dervishes. They were always in constant motion, and they always seemed to know where each other was going to be. One of them faked a shot on me and passed to a wide-open brother standing beside the net all alone. 3-1. Immediately after, on the next shift, we scored to make it 3-2. Still lots of time to win this thing.

The whole game, there was this one woman, sitting by herself. She was about 55 or 60, and for the two periods that I was at that end of the rink, I could hear her yelling at Darren Lucier. "Lucier you stink!... Go home Lucier!... Lucier, you're an embarrassment!... You're a bum Lucier!" This went on non-stop, every time Lucier was on the ice. With about 5 minutes to go in the third, we iced the puck. As the linesman retrieved the puck from the other end of the ice, our team lined up for the face off. The rink was quiet. Lucier's spot at the faceoff was directly in front of this woman. She started in on him, "Lucier! You…." and that's all she got out. I guess Darren had had enough abuse for one game, he yelled back at the top of his lungs, and he was ten times louder than she was, "SHUT YOUR MOUTH OR I'LL STICK MY COCK IN IT!!!" The whole rink, me included, were stunned. The woman stood up, grabbed her purse, turned to her left and walked out the exit at that end of the building. I don't know who she was, I never asked. Darren didn't know either and didn't have a clue what her problem with him was. I often wondered. We never saw or heard from her ever again.

For the last five minutes of the game, our team threw everything at the Hornets net, but we just couldn't get that tying goal. The game ended 3-2. The two teams shook hands and headed for the dressing room. The entry hall to the dressing room was behind the bench. As I got to the bench, the fans who had travelled from Assiniboia had gathered around the entryway and were clapping and hooting and saying stuff like "Great game Jerry!" There were maybe 15 of them. I gave them a quick smile and a nod and ducked into the dressing room. The room had a weird vibe. Most of the team and the coaches were kind of happy and unhappy at the same time. This was the first game that the Rebels hadn't been blown out, in fact, we were very close to winning. But a loss is a loss, and you just can't be happy with a loss. A couple of the executive guys came in and talked to Kim and a few of the players, congratulating them on a great game. Most of the guys dropped by my stall to shake my hand, some of them introduced themselves. The executive guys told me I had played great. I felt like a bit of a fraud. I knew that I had played well and made some solid saves… but in my heart, I knew that I had gotten lucky more than a few times. The score could have easily been 9-2, and I would've been home on Tuesday. But also, it was exhilarating. My first game of serious hockey. A lot of these guys had played in the Saskatchewan Junior League, and some had even played in the Western Hockey League. I was proud and ashamed all at the same time. Kim called me to come see him outside the dressing room and said that they had decided to sign me for the rest of the year. I shook his hand, and he told me that they would have a contract made up, and that I was to go to the Sporting Goods Store and see Frank on Monday. I told him no problem and went to get showered and dressed. I had some soul searching to do.

I didn't sleep much that night. I was seriously considering not signing and going home. A teacher in high school taught me that whenever I had a decision to make, get a piece of paper, draw a line down the middle, write "Pro" on one side and "Con" on the other. Then write all the good things about the decision on the pro side and all the bad things on the con side. Weigh the two against each other and come to a decision. I did this but it didn't help. I finally wrote a question at the bottom of the page. The question was, "Honestly. Can I play at this level?" I went back and forth on it. On the one hand, I made some really good saves during the game. On the other hand, if I signed and wasn't as good as I thought I was, I could become a real laughingstock. The decision came down to one thing. I was not going to get this opportunity again, and I would be letting myself down, (and Randy and John too) if I didn't take it. So, I decided to throw caution to the wind and sign.

CHAPTER 15

Neckties, Contracts, High Voltage

Next morning, I woke up and had breakfast. It wasn't time to go to the sporting goods store yet, so I went to pick up the local paper. I was interested in seeing what they had to say about the game. Turned out the paper only came out once a week. I looked at the sports section, and they just had an article about all the new players in town. They called me, "Jay Hack" My first "ink" and they get my name wrong. I decided to head to Frank's. I showed up at the shop and waited. One of the other guys who just got into town was in the office with Frank. After they were done, I went in. Frank again said that I had a great game. I just said thank you and didn't say anything else. "So, let's talk turkey," Frank said. I told him I loved turkey. He thought that was funny. I sat down and he put the contract in front of me. I remember it was on green paper, which I found odd. He explained it wasn't really a contract. It wouldn't be registered with the league or anyone else. It was just a legally binding agreement between the Rebels and me. It had a code of conduct on it, basically it just said don't be a fuckin' idiot. And in return for practicing and playing games, I would be paid $1000.00 a month, with a $100 stipend for room and board. $1,100.00 a month! I nearly shit myself. Along with my unemployment benefits, I was going to do pretty well. Frank said that they had found a place for me to stay as well. It would be in the basement suite of one of the local players. Tim Nickel had played in the Saskatchewan Junior League. He played one year with Willie Desjardins, who would one day coach my beloved Canucks. Tim's best friend was Doug Smail, who was playing for the Winnipeg Jets at the time. Tim was a teacher in town and was about 30 years old. He was married with two children, a boy and a girl. I don't remember his wife's name, but she was super nice and a good cook. Room and board would be about $250 a month Frank said, and there was going to be another player staying there as well. Rob Wallace was also from Burnaby, and had played in the BC Junior League with the Richmond Sockeyes. He was a defenseman who could skate really well and stop on a dime, allowing him to shake a check like nobody's business. Rob and I met each other for the first time at Tim Nickel's house. He seemed alright, not real talkative but a nice enough guy.

After looking over the contract, I signed it after reading the first line. "This agreement can be broken at any time by either party." Good enough for me. Since the month was already a week old, December's pay would be prorated, and I would get my full salary, every month, for the rest of the year, as long as neither party broke the agreement. Frank and I shook hands and that was that. I was unofficially, a professional hockey player! I thought about what I was going to tell John.

I moved in to Tim's basement, and we ran into an immediate problem. There was only one bedroom. Outside of the bedroom in this kind of anteroom, there was another bed. Then there was a bathroom, laundry room and living room. Since I was there first, I took the bedroom, and Rob took the bed in the anteroom. It turned out, Rob was an early to bed, early to rise type of guy, while I was a night owl, who liked to watch tv until 2 or 3 in the morning and then sleep late. Rob was also the lightest sleeper I have ever known. He would wake up if a mouse farted. He couldn't sleep when I was watching tv at night, so we decided to switch. He would take the bedroom, and I would sleep in the anteroom. The best thing about this arrangement was the bed in the anteroom was the most comfortable bed that I had ever slept on. This arrangement however, didn't work out either. I would be up watching "Naked City",(no, it's not porn). I would have the volume down so low I could only hear about half of what was being said. I had to sit directly in front of the tv. Rob would come in 2 or 3 times and turn it down. His bedroom was a good 20 feet away from the tv, and he had the door closed. I don't know how Rob could hear it because I couldn't hear what they were saying, and I was about 2 feet away, so it became a useless endeavour. I started reading books instead. I read Herman Wouk's "Winds of War", and "War and Remembrance" back to back. They became two of my favourite books ever. Rob was not exactly a considerate tenant. He had a habit of wearing a t-shirt that had a picture of Garfield the cat with the caption, "Sometimes you just gotta say what the fuck." Tim and his wife were Christians, and they had two young children. I asked Tim if the shirt offended him, and he kind of shrugged and said that if the children were old enough to read, he would ask Rob not to wear it. I told Tim that I would handle it. I told Rob he might want to reconsider his choice of wardrobe when he was at home. He said he hadn't even thought about it, but that he wouldn't wear that shirt anymore. I told him that was a good idea. Rob turned out to be kind of abrasive and not the best roommate, but he was a really good defenseman.

Chapter 16

Business Time

When you play Senior hockey, you practice way more than you play. I came to practice with the attitude that I was going to get better and not have to rely on luck to get me through the season. A surefire way to improve or implode, is to play against players who are better than you and pretty much everybody on the team was better than me. The next game we were on the road in Milestone to play the Flyers. First order of business was to find a cage that I liked. I had to give Bingo back his. I found one in the sportshop that was like Dominik Hasek's, it actually had eye holes that I could look directly through with no head gymnastics, so I was all set. The Flyers had a player named Darren Bobyck who had played for the Regina Pats in the Western League. He had scored over a hundred points in his last year. I was told to watch for him, he would be the player in the white skates. The Rebels were now zero wins and eleven losses, and with all the new faces, ("History" was now indeed, history), everyone associated with the team was hoping for our first win. It was a good game. I played well and my luck was holding out, and we skated to an 8-5 win. A couple of the executive guys were there. One of them, Howard Weal, came into the room and yelled, "You're all a bunch of fuckin' winners!" We all laughed. It was party time. One of our players, Rob Hrytsak, (pronounced HURTsack), scored four goals. Rob came to us from Saskatoon, and he still had professional aspirations. He was the type of player who would score five goals in a game and then disappear for a couple of games and then score six out of nowhere. Definitely the best player I ever played with. He left our team later that year to join the Johnstown Chiefs, (where they filmed the movie Slap Shot), of the East Coast Hockey League. He was even coached by one of the Hanson Brothers; Steve Carlson. The next time we played Milestone, this time at home, Rob got kicked out of the game in the first period for fighting. It wasn't much of a fight. The guy wasn't exactly hellfire on skates. Rob and him dropped their gloves, and Rob proceeded to ragdoll the guy. I don't think the guy even got a punch in. Turned out the guy was the Flyers bus driver, he didn't even play on the team. They remembered Rob had scored four goals on them the previous game, so he was sent out there just to start a fight with Rob and get him out of the game.

Another player who joined our team was Mark Davis. He was from Flin Flon, Manitoba. If you're ever to meet anybody from Flin Flon, you can assume this one thing. They are as tough as nails. Mark had a nickname, it was "Krinkle". I don't know where he got it from, or what it meant, but it didn't stick, not in Assiniboia. Everyone called him "Chili". Chili Davis was a popular baseball player at the time, so Mark became "Chili". It stuck like Velcro. I never saw Chili lose a fight. He took some lumps, but he always gave better than he got. I saw him get knocked to his knees once, but he just jumped up to his feet and started feeding the guy. He also was a sniper of the first order. He would skate down the right wing and let go a cannon off the far post and in. He just had that knack. The fans loved him, and he was by far the most popular player on the team. Chili told me this one story which is a favourite of mine. He was playing for the Brandon Wheat Kings as a seventeen-year old. Playing for them was a relative term, as he was on the roster, but he didn't get much playing time. He was always stapled to the end of the bench. That was until the Wheat Kings were on their western road swing. Every team in the Western League goes on one road trip a year to play all the teams in the other division. Brandon was in Victoria playing the Cougars. Chili was at the end of the bench as usual. Victoria had a powerhouse team that year, and Brandon was losing. Chili got a tap on the shoulder, and the coach told him to "make something happen". Chili got on the ice and on the first chance he had, he made a beeline for the goalie. He skated in hard and BOOM! He nailed the goalie, sending him flying ten or fifteen feet away. I said previously that in hockey, the goalie is untouchable and that there are consequences to even looking at him the wrong way. Turns out the goalie for the Cougars on this night was future Hall of Famer Grant Fuhr. Chili said that nineteen-year old Torrie Robertson (who went on to have a solid career in the NHL as a tough guy) picked him up and just threw haymakers at him. He ended up losing his top two front teeth. He would pull out the bridge and show us, just to prove his story.

I think we played a couple more games and won them both. My luck was holding out. The puck just seemed to hit me most of the time. But then the time came to play the powerful Moose Jaw Generals. This was going to be a litmus test. Pretty much all the Generals had played at a very high level. They were led by Jim Misener, their leading scorer. He had played in the Manitoba Junior league and had a couple years of pro experience down in the U.S. The Generals had a reputation as being a really tough team. They would annihilate you on the scoreboard, and then beat you down if you pissed them off. It was not pretty. Apparently, the hockey Gods, on this day anyway, were on the Generals side. Whatever good fortune I had had up to that point, was gone. I looked like a beer leaguer playing against pros. They had scored six on me by the five-minute mark of the second period. My luck had left me, and I got yanked. Bingo had left the team by then, so Chris was my backup. I felt sorry for the kid. I felt like I was throwing him to the wolves, but surprisingly, Chris played awesome. He made some highlight reel saves and kept the score from becoming an embarrassment. I think it ended up 9-4. One thing was obvious, I still had a lot to learn. The realization struck me that they weren't paying me to play, they were paying me to play well. I had to learn in a hurry.

Another good team in the league was the Fort Qu'Appelle Lakers. Fort Qu'Appelle is a beautiful little town northeast of Regina. It actually has a ski-hill, I think it's the only one in Saskatchewan. The Lakers weren't quite as good as the Generals, but they were close. They had two former Canucks playing for them. Drew Callender and Rob Tudor were actually teammates on my beloved Canucks for one season. I didn't have a lot of respect for Callender as he was an absolute sniper, but he seemed to only try if he had a chance to score. He didn't backcheck and rarely got into puck battles. He just waited for the puck to come to him. Tudor on the other hand, was the opposite. He was as hard-nosed as you can get. He scrapped, and clawed and fought for every inch of ice. Every time we played against them Tudor had two black eyes. They also had a defenseman who had allegedly played for the National Team, but I don't remember his name. I think his last name was Raedeke. We played them well, but lost 6-3. I didn't play particularly well, but I remember that during this game, the play seemed to finally slow down for me. For the first time, I didn't have that "playing in a blender" feeling.

Between the games and practicing, I was slowly making the adjustment. I really struggled for a few more games, but as the season wore on, we started winning more than we were losing. In fact, we were beating everyone except Moose Jaw and Fort Qu'Appelle. The games against Gravelbourg were always close, and we were probably .500 against them. The new guys were making an impact, and the local guys were playing well. It was a good combination, and most of the guys got along.

We had one more game against the Generals. They had basically run roughshod over the whole league, leaving bodies in their wake. This last time that we played them, they came to Assiniboia with eight players. Sometimes, in senior hockey you had to play with a short bench. Injuries, work, previous engagements, players coming and going, can wreak havoc on your roster. If we were ever going to beat the Generals, this was going to be our golden opportunity. Their goalie, Martin Wood, had apparently left the team and their backup goalie was from Assiniboia. Ravi Tanna was the type of goalie you see every once in a while. He would make some absolutely impossible saves, and then let in a dribbler from center ice. Stop all the hard ones and let in the easy ones. Once the game got started, it was back and forth. They would score, we would score. It went that way the whole game until the very end. The final buzzer went, and we had won, 10-9. It was a wild and crazy game and was about to get wilder and crazier. The Generals started a brawl. They had eight players, and they wanted to brawl. There was about five of our players that had no interest in fighting. One of our defensemen, Del Byron, was a cop in town, and there was no way in hell that he was going to get involved. The rest of our guys were more than happy to accommodate our friends from Moose Jaw. The rivalry between Moose Jaw and Assiniboia was intense.

It starts with the youngest kids and goes all the way to the adults. In sports, Assiniboia hates Moose Jaw and vice versa. One of the Generals players, who was already suspended, came out of the stands and ran around to our bench to take on our coach, (this player would be suspended for life after this incident), Kim Waiting. Kim obliged him and gave as good as he got. Then Kim and the assistant coach went on the ice, trying to get our players into the dressing room. They didn't want any of our players getting suspended so close to the playoffs. The Generals player who was already suspended stood up on the boards at our bench and grabbed on to a water pipe that ran above, along the length of the bench. He hung on to the pipe and was kicking at our players that came near him. It was pandemonium. Ravi was about half my size and neither one of us had any interest in fighting. I went and stood beside him. We chatted and watched the festivities. For the second (and last) time in my life, I was involved in a bench clearing brawl, and I had the best seat in the house.

Order was finally restored and the teams went to their respective dressing rooms. No handshake today. In our dressing room, it was high fives all around. We had given the Generals a dose of their own medicine. They were a cocky bunch of fucks, and we had beaten them at their own game. Of course, had they had their whole team, it would've been a different story, but you can only play the team in front of you. And we had won! Apparently, the referees hated the Generals as much as we did. Not one of our players was suspended. The game report said that the Generals had instigated everything, and we had just defended ourselves. Winner winner chicken dinner.

There are two sets of playoffs in senior hockey. The league playoffs, where you play only teams in your own league. And then the S.A.H.A. provincial playoffs. You designate which level you want to play, Senior A, AA, or AAA. Senior A only goes as far as provincial championships, whereas AA and AAA go as far as national championships, the Hardy Cup and the Allan Cup respectively. The team executive decided we would enter the AA playdowns. The first round we had to play the Fort Qu'Appelle team. They had added a couple of players for the S.A.H.A. playoffs. They were a formidable opponent. We were able to keep up, but in the end, we lost two straight. The games were something like 5-1, 6-3. I got a big compliment from the Fort Qu'Appelle coach. He had told our coach that I was a "gamer". I couldn't believe that of all our players, he had singled me out for such high praise. I was grateful. And I finally felt like I belonged. That, even though I had no junior experience, I deserved to be there and I could hold my own with anyone and that I wasn't a fraud. Howard Mehain and I would tell the story of my first phone calls to him many times and laugh and shake our heads.

We still had the league playoffs to go. Our first opponent was Gravelbourg. We had actually won enough games to get home ice advantage. They would come to us first. The first game was close. Each team gave everything they had. In the end Komonoski was the difference. We lost 4-3. Bad thing was, in the third period I went to my knees to make a save and heard a pop. I felt no pain, just a pop. I finished the game but right after, my knee swelled up like crazy. I got ice on it right away. The next day I could hardly walk. The next game was in three days. I did everything I could to get the swelling down. Rest, ice, compression, elevation. By the time game day came, the swelling had gone down, but it still hurt like hell. In the dressing room before the game, I had it taped, wrapped, and braced. I could only bend it straight back. There was no way I was going to be able to butterfly. I managed to play the whole game, but we lost 4-1. The season was over. Turned out

I had a sprained medial collateral ligament. It would take six weeks to heal.

At the end of season banquet, I won Rookie of the Year, and also Best Goalie. The best goalie one I felt a little queasy about. It was only me and Chris, and I had played almost all of the games. I felt there really shouldn't be an award for that.

Some memories of that first season: Everyone in Saskatchewan smokes. At least it seems that way. If you met a non-smoker, it was a rarity. I think it was the law, everybody who is a citizen of Saskatchewan must smoke or face a fine.

Everybody's a farmer. In the big city, when you meet somebody for the first time, inevitably you will ask them what they do for a living. It's a conversation starter. For the first while after I got to town and I met someone new, I would ask what they did for a living. Every time they would reply, "I'm a farmer." After a few weeks, I stopped asking. If the conversation lapsed, I would ask, "So how big is your farm?"

Dave Venn, one of our forwards, came from Calgary. He started dating a girl from Moose Jaw. It turned out she was one of the "bar-chicks" that had boarded the train with me in Maple Ridge. She and her friend who was with her on the train, started hanging out with the team in Assiniboia regularly. They turned out to be a lot of fun. They recognized me from the train and laughed about my boots.

In Saskatchewan it gets fucking cold! We would practice in the arena when it was -40°C outside. My sweat would freeze to my jersey until there was a thick layer of ice. Every once in awhile someone would hit me there with a shot and the whole thing would smash into little shards. God help me if I got some in my eye. Not only would it be painful from the impact, but the salt would stay in my eye for an hour after.

One time I walked home from a party when it was this cold. I only had to walk three blocks, but I only had a light jacket on, and I, literally, barely made it. My forehead was absolutely frozen solid. If I would've had another block to go, I doubt I would've survived. I never tried that again.

A friend of Dave Venn, a guy named Kevin came to town to play for the Rebels. He was supposed to replace Rob Hyrtsak after Rob had left to join the Johnstown Chiefs (Who own da Chiefs?). He wasn't nearly as good as Rob, but he was okay. The guy knew a million jokes. Kevin could go on forever telling joke after joke. It was quite a talent. While in town, he had stayed at the same hotel that I had stayed at. Since he was only going to be in town for a month or two, the team decided not to board him with anyone. By the end of the season he had run up a $300.00 tab at the Bar-B. When the season ended, he was going to pay the tab with his last cheque from the team. After room and board, his cheque would've been about $700.00. But his girlfriend lived back in Calgary, and he had spent so much time talking to her on the phone, his phone bill came to $690.00. He got a cheque from the team for $10.00. He wrote a letter to the Bar-B saying how embarrassed he was, and that he would pay the tab as soon as he got back to Calgary and made some money. I don't know if he ever paid it off, I'm assuming he did, he seemed like a good guy.

To raise money for the team, occasionally we would sponsor a Bingo in Moose Jaw. All the players who were available were expected to help out by working the floor. Selling cards, dabbers and helping anyone who needed it. It shocked me how serious bingo players were about the game. God help you if you called out "Bingo", and it wasn't a bingo. The crowd would turn on you and threaten to take you out back and beat the shit out of you. I was working the non-smoking section, (which seemed to have more smoke that the smoking section), and I was talking to this sweet young lady of about 70. She wasn't having any luck with her numbers. She requested that I do something about it. I asked her if she wanted me to have a word with the bingo caller. She said, and I quote, "I want you to slit his throat." That, my friends, is some serious Bingo-ing. True story.

The Rebel fans were amazing. Saskatchewan people are the best. They took me in with open arms and made me feel at home. We had about 300 ardent fans and a bunch of more casual fans. I wasn't the most popular player on the team, but I was close. I could never buy my own drink in the bar. There were always invitations to come over to supper. Anything that I needed, people would bend over backwards to get it for me. People would stop me in the street and want to talk hockey. It was great. But I'm a city boy. Small town life is very different from city life. For one, in the city, people tend to mind their own business. In a small town, everybody knows what everybody else is doing and with whom. The rumour mill does double time. There was a rumour about me sleeping with a girl that I hadn't even met. It takes some getting used to, and after awhile you just ignore it. People will believe whatever they want. But the experience was, for the vast majority of time, very positive. I wouldn't trade my time in Assiniboia for anything. It was probably the best time of my life.

CHAPTER 17

A Season in Hell

I returned back home to the city about a week after the season ended and went back to working for a living. I returned to my paving stone job and made sure I got my 20 weeks in so I could get unemployment benefits again.

During this summer, I entered a rock trivia contest at a nightclub. I have an uncanny ability to remember useless information. Everything important goes right out the window, but if it's trivia it will stick in my brain forever. The contest was set up like Jeopardy! It had gone on for four weeks, and the same two guys had won twice each. I entered on the fifth week and neither of those guys were there. I won the preliminary round that night and qualified for the semi-final and final to be held the following week. In the first semi-final, I was up against one of the two guys that had won twice in the preliminary rounds. He was really strange. One of those guys who thinks they're really funny, but they just make you roll your eyes. The other contestant was a girl who was super nervous. I won that round and made it to the final. The other semi-final was won by the other guy who had won twice in the preliminary rounds. Apparently the two guys were best buddies and figured they had stacked the deck in their favour. They hadn't counted on me (the king of useless information) being there. It's me and this other guy, who seemed almost normal compared to his friend, in the final. You had to get 10 questions right. He got the first one right, and I got the second one wrong. Which put him up by two. I reeled off a few in a row, but then he got a couple. We went back and forth like that until I was leading 9-7. The next question came and it was, "What instrument does Patrick Moraz play?" I knew the answer and buzzed in, but too late. The other guy was a little quicker this time. I looked over at him and could tell that he wasn't sure of the answer. I whispered to him, "You better get it right." He answered, "Trumpet!". BZZZZZZT. The host asked me if I knew, and I said, "keyboards!" I knew that Patrick Moraz was the keyboardist for The Moody Blues. I won! I got to see the concert of my choice with ten of my friends. We would watch it from the Coca-Cola gallery suite (they had sponsored the contest) in the Pacific Coliseum. We got limousine service to and from the show, free dinner and drinks, as well as t-shirts and all sorts of Coca-Cola swag. We saw Eric Clapton who had Mark Knopfler from Dire Straits playing guitar for him. The opening act was a band called Buckwheat Zydeco, and they were awesome. One guy in the band actually played the washboard. It was a great night. The girl who ran the contest was in the limo with us, and she said that she was so happy that one of those other guys didn't win. She said they were creepy as hell and couldn't imagine having to spend an evening with them. I was glad she approved of me.

The 1988/89 season was scheduled to start at the end of October. Before that, in September the Rebels were scheduling their first ever Hockey School. They wanted me to come to Assiniboia and be an instructor. I got my 20 weeks in just a week prior so I got there the night before the first ice time. I had been to Vic's Goalie School one time for a week about 3 years prior. I remembered a few of the drills that they had us perform but, other than that, I was entirely self-taught. I learned by watching others. If I had to describe my style it would be "hybrid," because I took a little bit of everyone I had ever watched and incorporated it into my game. Teaching somebody else would be very difficult, if not impossible for me. The saving grace was that the Gravelbourg Hornets had folded, and we snagged some of their players. Including two of the three Gaucher brothers. We got one of their defensemen, Glen Knutson, and the best goalie in the league, Darren Komonoski. He was to be my goaltending partner that year. I couldn't have been happier. I was going to be able to pick his brain and learn some new tricks. He would instruct the goalies at the hockey school, and I would assist him. Basically, I got to go to goalie school for free. I learned just as much as the kids did.

The hockey school was a huge success and lots of kids came from all over Southern Saskatchewan. A lot of the Rebel players instructed and we seemed to win over a lot of new fans.

When the hockey school ended, we still had a month to go before the season began which meant no paychecks were coming in. It took awhile before my unemployment checks would start arriving. Komo and I got a temporary job at the golf course and were tasked with getting it ready for winter. I didn't even know that Assiniboia had a golf course. We made enough money to tide us over until the season started.

I was hoping that I could board with Tim and his wife again that year, but they had separated, and it just wasn't possible. I asked Tim if I could buy the bed that I liked off of them, but he said they wanted to hang on to it. Bummer. Darren Lucier and I decided to rent a house together. Bobby Helland, one of the local players on the team had gotten married over the summer and was renting out his old house for $200 a month. Lucier and I became roommates for the season. Our house became "party central". After the bar closes, people would stick around and find out where the afterparty was going to be. Quite often it would be at our house. On one occasion, Lucier was out of town and these three girls were wanting me to let everyone party at our house. I felt very uncomfortable with the situation, because they were the only three people that I knew that were still in the bar, everybody else was a total stranger to me. They begged me until I finally acquiesced. About twenty-five people came to my house, twenty-two of them I didn't know. The same three girls who had begged me to host the party, left about twenty minutes after they got there. So, I was left with a houseful of strangers. It lasted about another fourty minutes and then I asked everyone to leave. Luckily, there were no assholes amongst the group and they left peacefully. The next day, one of the three girls dropped by in the late morning to invite me for lunch (or dinner, or whatever), but I already had plans. She apologized for the three of them and said they would make it up to me. I made it clear that I wasn't happy but no harm, no foul. I made sure that I held it over their heads for a couple of months. I can be quite good at guilt trips.

There were big changes in the league as well. The Generals were gone. Times were hard and money became tighter. Their sponsorship had evaporated and they couldn't afford to import players. All of their players would now be local, and they would be called the Pla-Mors, (Playmores). Don't ask me what the name means. I researched it, and nobody seems to know. All I know is that the name had originated many years ago. They would still have a competitive team, but they would be far from the powerhouse they had been. Also gone were the Milestone Flyers, and in their place would be the Regina Blackhawks. Darren Bobyck and all the best players from the Flyers would play on this team as well as some pickups from Regina. Fort Qu'Appelle was gone as well. It would be Assiniboia, Weyburn, Regina, Balgonie and Moose Jaw.

Our team was much improved. After adding the Gravelbourg guys, we also added some top-notch speed. Scott Binner had speed to burn. He was 21 years old and was doing an accounting apprenticeship at Frank's sporting goods store. Scott probably could've been a world class speed skater if he had chosen to go that route, but he loved hockey just as much as I did. The rumour was that he had a tryout with the Moose Jaw Warriors of the Western League, and they immediately put him on a line with Thoeren Fleury because he was the only one who could keep up with him. He didn't make the team, but the experience was invaluable. Scott described Fleury as a "cocky little fuck". Scott had this deceptive skating style and would skate up the wing and by the time the defenseman figured out what was happening, Scott was by him. Sometimes after games, Scott's forearms would have nasty red welts on them where the defensemen would slash him as he went by. Scott wasn't a gifted goal scorer, but he scored enough. His speed just gave him so many opportunities. A great guy too. Easy to laugh, and if he said he was going to do something, he did it. Scott didn't need a nickname, everybody just called him Binner. I don't think I ever heard anyone call him Scott. He was Binner. I once had dinner with him and his parents at his house in Assiniboia. I entered the kitchen and they were all sitting there. I looked at Scott and said, "Hey Binner." I then shook his dad's hand and said, "Binner." I then turned to his mom and said, "Binner." They thought it was funny, even if you don't. We also added Curtis Marcenko and the Sandbeck brothers, Grant and Kelly. Curtis was, pound for pound, the toughest guy I ever met. He was about 5' 6" tall and maybe a buck forty-five. But he would take on guys twice his size and more than hold his own. Grant Sandbeck always reminded me of Don Luce, the old time Buffalo Sabre who could drive teams crazy with his defensive play. Kelly Sandbeck was a solid winger who could play the game really well at both ends of the rink. Both of the Sandbecks smiled a lot, and were great guys to have on the team.

Just before the season began, I was called into the coach's office. The new coach was Jerry Volsky. He had coached in minor hockey and had a lot of success with the Bantams, and Kim Waiting would be his assistant coach this year. Art Birss was the new GM of the team, with Howard Mehain assuming different duties. Art and Jerry, whose nickname was "Chick," were in the office. Art explained that they were only going to pay $100 a game this year, and since we only played maybe 6 or 8 games a month, it would be a big cut in pay. I was ok with it. I was still getting paid to play hockey and $600 or $800 goes a long way in Assiniboia. Then they gave me the bad news. They said the team could only afford to pay that to one goalie, and that was going to be Komo. My nobody status struck again. Not having a reputation or a resume can really suck sometimes. They told me the "backup" goalie would be paid $50 a game. I did some quick math in my head and figured that I could not live on $50 a game. I told them that I would have to go home. They said ok. I walked out of the room almost in tears when it dawned on me. I had totally forgotten about my unemployment benefits. I went back in the room and told them I had changed my mind, and I would sign for the $50 a game. They seemed like they didn't care one way or the other, they just said ok.

When October came around, we played a few exhibition games before the start of the season. After one of these games, I was in the Bar-B and noticed a cute blonde girl with big hair walk into the place. She was with a few friends. She didn't look around, just went straight to a seat and sat down. I asked around if anyone knew who she was, but nobody did. After some time passed, I went against my instincts and sat down beside her. I asked her very bluntly, "Who are you?" which she thought was funny. We ended up talking the rest of the night. Her name was Terrie, and she was from Gravelbourg. She had a great sense of humour and was one of those girls who didn't need makeup to look good. She had freckles, but you could barely see them. She was only 18 and was hoping not to get her identification checked. A stand-up comedian I once saw said, "If you can't get the laugh, go for the gross out." Terrie actually put this into practice, and would say really gross things about her friend's food. I fell in love immediately. We would be together for the next five years. She was very mature for her age, and sometimes I would forget how young she was. One time we were driving to Moose Jaw to see her sister when the song, "I've Got My Mind Set on You," by George Harrison came on the radio. After it was over, she said, "George Harrison? Wasn't he in a band?" I couldn't believe my ears. "HE WAS IN THE FUCKING BEATLES!! MY GOD, YOU ARE YOUNG!!" I resisted the urge to pull over and make her walk the rest of the way.

We went to a party while we were in Moose Jaw, and I actually bumped into History, (I never did find out what his real name was). We got to talking about the Rebels. He was still deluded into thinking he was a great hockey player. He said to me, "Yeah, I had the skill to play for the Rebels, I just didn't have the size." I resisted the urge to point out that we had Grant Sandbeck, Curtis Marcenko, and Kent Blythe playing on the team and that they were the same size, if not smaller, than he was. He made me think of Lonnie, the goalie for the Burnaby Kings who thought he was the second coming of Jacques Plante. Who was I to burst his bubble? I just agreed with him, and I never saw History after that.

The big news for that season was that we were going to Fairbanks, Alaska to play a team up there. The Alaska Gold Kings. Exciting times.

In league games, it was basically us and the Blackhawks. Weyburn, Balgonie, and Moose Jaw were about the same caliber wise at the bottom of the standings. The Blackhawks and us were pretty even at the top. Komo played about two thirds of the games. Since they were paying him twice as much as me, they wanted to get their money's worth. I wasn't too concerned, Komo and I got along really well, and I was learning a lot from him.

A couple of weeks before Christmas, Jerry Volsky invited the whole team down to his cabin for a snowmobile party. Almost the whole team went and at least half of them owned snowmobiles. Being from Vancouver, I had never driven a snowmobile, or even been a passenger on one. Kevin Silzer took me for a ride and showed me the basics. It seemed easy enough. After going back and sitting by the fire for awhile, Terrie asked Kevin if she and I could borrow his ski-doo and go for a ride. Kevin was pretty drunk by then, and I think he would've signed over his house if Terrie had asked him to. So off we went. It was probably -20 out and there wasn't a lot of snow but enough to snowmobile on. I climbed on and Terrie got on behind me. I took it pretty slow for the first while and didn't want to go too far. It would've been easy to get lost. The moon was full, and we sped up along this ridge. It was a beautiful night. We found a spot where the snow was quite a bit deeper, and I decided to stop and enjoy the view. Terrie immediately exclaimed, "What are you doing?!! You can't stop!" I thought she was kidding. "Why can't we stop?" "Because you'll get stuck!!" I said, "It's a fucking snowmobile!!

How does it get stuck in the fucking snow?!!" She laughed and said, "They can!" We tried to get going again and sure enough, we were stuck. She got off and immediately sank to her mid-thighs in the deep snow. Luckily, she was wearing a snowsuit. I just had jeans on. I told her to go back to the ridge where the snow wasn't so deep, and she trudged her way up there. I got off and tried to lift the back end of the snowmobile, got back on and tried to go. I got about ten feet. I repeated the process about ten times until finally I got to some shallower snow and was able to get some traction. I was absolutely soaked with sweat and melted snow, and I was exhausted. We went back to the cabin and sat inside until I dried off. We didn't tell anyone about our little adventure. The next day I was so sore, I couldn't move. I haven't ridden a snowmobile since.

When my roommate, Darren Lucier, learned that I wasn't going home for Christmas that year, he insisted that I come home with him. He was from Hudson Bay which was in Northern Saskatchewan. The day after the last game before Christmas, we left in Darren's Dodge Daytona, (piece of shit car). Late in the afternoon, we arrived in Hudson Bay. In Southern Saskatchewan, there aren't very many trees. Most of the ones you see have been planted in a row to help with soil erosion, but when you get to a certain point in the north, you enter into forest country all of a sudden. Hudson Bay had trees everywhere. I thought it was beautiful. I met Darren's parents, Sadie and Leo, they were lovely people, and made me feel at home right away. As well as his younger brother Darwin, and his sister Melanie. They were very welcoming, and we all had a wonderful Christmas together. Except for Darwin insisting we watch eight hours of homemade wrestling videos. He was a huge WWF fan, and he and his friends made these amateur videos of themselves wrestling in someone's basement. If you are reading this Darwin, that was excruciating! Darren was friends with Chicago Blackhawks defenseman, Trent Yawney, who was also from Hudson Bay. He had played at the 1988 Olympics in Calgary and was now playing for the Chicago Blackhawks. I think he was injured at the time, which is why he was home at Christmas. We had a short visit with him. I asked him about Andy Moog and Sean Burke, who were the two Olympic goalies. He said that they were both great guys but hyper competitive, and that they didn't really get along that well. We also asked him about Mike Keenan. We had heard through the grapevine that he was an asshole, and we were wondering if that was true or not. He told us Mike Keenan was a huge dick, and a huge dick for no reason. It was a great Christmas, and one that I will never forget. Sadie, Melanie, Darwin, and another sister Michelle, who wasn't there that Christmas, still live in Hudson Bay. Darren lives in Calgary. Sadly, Leo died in a car accident in 1990. R.I.P Leo. I will never forget your kindness.

In early January we got a taste of international play. Over Christmas, there was an international junior tournament in Saskatoon. Art Birss and the executive board had managed to set up two exhibition games with teams that had played in that tournament. Jan. 3, 1989 we would play the St. Paul Vulcans and Jan. 5th we would play a Swedish junior team. Chick told me I would play the first game against the St. Paul team. The St. Paul Vulcans from Minnesota played in the U.S.H.L. Phil Housley, Tim Jackman and Trent Klatt had all played for the Vulcans at various times. When gameday came, the town pulled out all the stops. They had an honour guard and the mayor of Assiniboia, Carl Pilkey, dropped the puck for the ceremonial faceoff. It was quite the show. The game was sold out, it was "standing room only". When the game started, I had that feeling of playing in a blender again.

Everything happened so fast. I didn't have time to think, which is probably a good thing. Thinking has never been my strong suit. We were playing a very good team which had no weak or even average players. This was a serious hockey team. All I could do was react because there was seriously no time to think. If I let a rebound out, they would be all over it. Apparently, I was in my element. I ended up being awarded player of the game for our team. We won, 5-3 in a stunning upset. The shots were 39-23 for the Vulcans. "Live long and prosper" *(Mr. Spock, Star Trek 1966)*.

On Jan. 5th we played the Swedish team. Komo was scheduled to start this game but came down with a slight flu bug. He told me that I had to be ready to go in. They were a small skilled team. On average we probably outweighed them by 20 pounds. When the game started, it became obvious that the other team's players didn't really want to be there. They didn't put up much of a fight, and we beat them 9-4. Komo managed to play the whole game. The worst part was that they were sneaky dirty. They were always getting their sticks into the nether regions of our players. Our guys started to get a little frustrated by it. When the third period rolled around, we started hitting them. Our fans started to turn on us, thinking that we were roughing up a smaller, younger team. The fans couldn't see all the dirty stuff that was going on. Nothing really came of it, but don't think that just because someone is Swedish, they aren't capable of playing dirty pool. All in all, the two games were a highlight of the year, and a feather in our collective cap.

In February, we went on our longest road trip ever. We had a flight to Vancouver from Regina. From there the second leg to Whitehorse, where we would play their senior team on Thursday night, and then on to Fairbanks for the games on Friday and Saturday. Fairbanks had been in the middle of a cold snap. It got to -125°F a couple of weeks before we went. It was only -75°F in Fairbanks the morning we left. Saskatchewan was having its own cold blast at the time. We had to take the bus to Regina which was -45°C. With the wind chill it ended up being -70°C, which made it painful to be outside. We all met at the rink to board the bus. The heater on the bus worked, but it wasn't optimal. We all had to keep our winter jackets on, and I wasn't the only one wearing snow boots this time. We made it to Moose Jaw no problem, but going from Moose Jaw to Regina we were driving straight into a headwind. By the time we got about 10 miles outside of Regina, the power steering fluid had frozen. Andy Tremblay, our bus driver, said he needed some help steering the bus. Kim Waiting and Kevin Silzer walked to the front of the bus and when the time came to turn onto the street that lead to the Regina airport, it took all three of them to crank the wheel. There was one more left turn into the airport. When we arrived, there was one porter outside watching us drive up. He started laughing when he saw three people driving the bus.

We made it to Vancouver. I called my family. We only had a two-hour layover so it wasn't worth it for anyone to come see me. Before we knew it, we were on our way to Whitehorse. That night we played the Kopper King Canadians, (there's that name again), and beat them 3-2. Komo and I split the game. We stayed in Whitehorse overnight and caught a morning flight to Fairbanks.

We flew on an old DC-3 which was built around 1940 we were told. A few of us were a little apprehensive to fly on such an old aircraft, but then they told us that the DC-3 had the best safety record of any airplane ever built which made us feel better. We landed in Fairbanks and went to the hotel. We had some time to kill before game time. Komo was going to play that night, and I would play the Saturday game. We got to the rink and got ready for the game. The best part about playing in Alaska was we were allowed to wear our "cats eye" masks. Since we weren't in Canada, we weren't under CSA jurisdiction. The Gold Kings were supposed to be a very good team. They had won the American equivalent of the Allan Cup a couple of times. The Moose Jaw Generals had come up in the past (and had a bench clearing brawl, surprise surprise) and the games were very close. The Gold Kings had a very vocal and raucous crowd, and there were about 2,000 of them. It was awesome. They were yelling and cursing and loud as hell. It made for an electric atmosphere. It soon became apparent that the Gold Kings had a stronger team than us. They outshot us pretty badly and Komo had to stand tall. When the Gold Kings went up 3-0, the whole crowd yelled in unison, "HEY GOALIE! WHAT'S THE SCORE?" They then would count out how many goals they had, "ONE, TWO THREE!" Then they would cheer (if they scored ten or more, they would count by fives. As you can imagine it would get pretty tiring counting after the tenth goal). They did this after every goal, (as long as they were winning). This was on top of all the abuse that was raining down on us. The first time you hear it, you can imagine what it's like being the goalie. The game ended something like 5-2, but it could have been much worse. I was going to be nervous when my turn came the next night.

After the game, I stayed at the hotel with my buddy Binner and a few of the others. Most of the other guys went to the local establishments. The next night, my turn came. The advantage of sitting on the bench the first game is that you can scout the team you're playing against. See what they do, how they do it. Pick out the good players that you're going to have to keep an eye on. The disadvantage to playing the second game is that most of our players are usually hungover and not at their best. Game time came. They played "Oh Canada" over the speakers. I had noticed the night before that there was a mistake in the song. The singer sang "True Patriots of," instead of "True Patriot Love." I thought it was strange that Americans, who would undoubtedly protest if their national anthem was misstated, couldn't get our national anthem right. Anyway, the game started, and it went pretty much the same as the night before. I got the, "HEY GOALIE" routine, but at least I was ready for it. We lost something like 6-2. After the game, we went to a bar. I think it was called "The Greyhound." The people were friendly but a little different. Fairbanks is fairly isolated, and they have a lot of military people there. The comedian Gallagher said the place was on the "road to nowhere" which I thought was apt. I guess growing up in such a place made you a little different. It was interesting to talk to the locals. In general, they were very direct, and there was no pussy footing around any subject. My "bullshit detector" read zero whenever I spoke to a local. The bar closed at 5:00 a.m., and we used every minute to party hard. As far as we knew, this would be our last time here, and we wanted to make the most of it. We had a 9:00 a.m. flight back to Whitehorse. Back on to the DC-3 for a couple of hours, then to Vancouver, Calgary, Saskatoon, and finally, Regina. Then we met Andy at the airport for the two-hour drive back to Assiniboia. I can see why NHLers hate airports. It is so monotonous having to wait around for your plane, especially if you have to make connecting flights.

Around this time, my roommate Lucier got a job offer in Calgary that was too good to turn down, and he left the team. I would miss him. We had a lot of good times together, and he was a great roomie. He was my first friend on the team, and he has the same stupid sense of humour that I have. He also had this ability to talk girls into coming over to our house and do our housework. I have pictures. I would visit him in Calgary on my way home after the season was over. We are still friends to this day.

Brian Wilkie was a former Regina Pat who had joined us from the University of Saskatchewan. He was taking a break from school, and Art recruited him to play for us in the interim. Brian was playing for the Pats in 1987 and was actually on the ice when Brad Hornung was cross checked into the boards and suffered a devastating spinal injury and became a quadriplegic. It was national news. To Brian, life was easy. He never seemed to lack for cash and always had a smile on his face. He was gregarious and good natured. On road trips, he would always get everyone singing these stupid little songs. One person would make up something, (usually an insult), rhyming with another person's name. Or he would make up word games for everyone to play. He was like our very own game show host. Everybody liked Brian. Wayne Resch was a 6' 4" centerman on our team. Wayne was not blessed with a lot of talent. He had actually been a goalie until he was 14 when he switched to forward. For us, he was a checker, and he did it well. Wayne never scored much, but he always potted the odd goal here and there. Brian had noticed that, at one point, Wayne had gone 10 games without scoring a goal. Before the 11th game, Brian yelled out that the Vegas oddsmakers put Wayne at 10-1 that he would score that game. Wayne didn't score. For the next part of the schedule, before every game, Brian would announce what the Vegas odds were that Wayne would score. Wayne was an extremely good-natured soul, who laughed along with everyone else about it, but the longer it went, you could tell he wanted to get that monkey off his back. We were playing Weyburn, and the odds got to 145 to 1 in the 16th game of the streak, when

Wayne finally scored on a rebound. The goal made the score 5-1 for us late in the 3rd period. Watching Wayne's reaction, you would've thought that he had just scored the Stanley Cup winning goal in the 7th game in overtime. He nearly jumped out of his equipment. The Devils had to be wondering what the fuck is wrong with this guy? The next game, Wilkie presented Wayne with a black t-shirt that read in bold letters, "SNIPER." It had a skeleton head with criss-cross bullet belts. Below that it said, "MESS WITH THE BEST, DIE LIKE THE REST." Wayne wore it with pride.

At a party we were at, Wilkie was chatting with a pretty blonde girl named Melissa for about 20 minutes when all of the sudden a guy walks over to him and without saying a word just busted him in the chops. Most hockey players when punched in the face in a social setting would strike back without a second's hesitation. Wilkie just grabbed the guy, turned him around and put him in a bear hug. He then asked the guy what his problem was. Turned out it was Melissa's ex-boyfriend, and he didn't like Wilkie talking to her. Wilkie did what he does best; diffuse the situation with humour and good will. A lesson all of us can learn. They ended up shaking hands, and what could've been an ugly situation became a non-issue. That was Wilkie.

We had about 5 games left in the season when Komo hurt his knee. It just locked up on him. He actually made a really good save while standing on his one good leg. He had suffered torn cartilage and would need surgery. His season was done. Since I arrived in Assiniboia for the first time, I had heard of this guy Mike Bloski. He was a bit of a goalie legend and kind of a "gun for hire." All the top senior teams recruited him to play for them. He had played junior for Saskatoon and Prince Albert of the Western League and had played a few years of pro. He even played a few games in the American Hockey

League for Hershey. I learned that he was going to be my new goaltending partner. He wouldn't be eligible for the league playoffs but would be for the S.A.H.A. provincial playoffs. Komo's exact words were, "the guy is good." I was anxious to meet him. The next day, we were in the dressing room getting ready for practice, and in walks this short, pudgy guy smoking a cigar. He was wearing a short-sleeved dress shirt and tie. If you can look like a slob wearing a shirt and tie, this guy pulled it off. He had an old army duffle bag with him that I assumed carried his hockey equipment. He walked up to Jerry Volsky and said, "Hi, Mike Bloski," and extended his hand. My first impression of him was, he was much less than I expected. When he dumped his equipment out, it was all at least 20 years old. He got dressed in like 5 minutes. In comparison, it took me a half hour, with all the extra pads that I had to attach to me. He didn't have any of that. We got onto the ice, and I went to introduce myself. He extended his hand and said, "You're Jerry Hack? Nice to meet you, Mike Bloski." The feeling of being a hockey nobody left me for a second. He was a really nice guy. Everybody liked him right away, Jerry Volsky especially. In fact, he was absolutely in love with the guy, or at least his resume. I wouldn't start another game for the rest of the regular season. I spent my time on the bench watching Bloski. He had a weird style and had this way of forcing opponents to shoot right at him. He was an expert at playing the percentages. His reflexes were sharp, and he had a really good glove hand. We won all five games that were left on the schedule, and I didn't play a minute. I had to keep in mind that Bloski wasn't eligible for the league playoffs, and I knew that I had to keep sharp.

The regular season ended, and we finished first, with Regina right behind us. Weyburn and Moose Jaw finished 3rd and 4th respectively. We had to play Moose Jaw in a best

2 out of 3 starting in our barn. Moose Jaw was a shadow of their former selves, and we had handled them with relative ease all season. I couldn't tell you how satisfying it was to hand them their lunch several times after they had done it to everyone else for so long. They still had some good players and one great one. Jim Misener still led the league in scoring despite playing for an inferior team. They had a couple more holdovers from the Generals days, but the rest were just "ham and eggers" to fill out the roster. The first game progressed, and we were winning 6-2 late in the game. A Moose Jaw player came over our blue line into the face-off circle and let go a slap shot. I did the splits, and the puck hit my pad just above my ankle. Another Moose Jaw player was bearing down on me, and when I was at my most vulnerable; he absolutely laid me out. By the time I got my bearings, I was laying on the ice, and the puck was within my reach. Before I could put my glove on it, the other Moose Jaw player swept it into the net. I looked at the referee, and he was pointing at the net indicating a goal. My first reaction after I got to my feet was to go after the referee. I realized however, that the guy who ran me was still laying there.

I should pause here and just let you know that I have a really bad temper. It doesn't rear its ugly head very often and very few people have seen me when I lose it. I can only describe it as "black rage." Just as an example, I was fixing a printer one day when I was living in my parent's basement. I had spent an hour fixing this stupid thing. All I had to do was get this one little tab back into place, and I would be finished. I worked at it for about 5 minutes trying to get this little tab in with sweat dripping down my face, and the tab snapped and broke. Years later, my dad was still finding pieces of that printer all over the basement.

When I noticed the guy was still laying there, I took my stick by the knob on the very end and with one hand whipped my stick over my head and down on this guy's ankle as hard as I could. It was like somebody trying one of those amusement-park games where you take a sledgehammer and hammer down on a little see-saw thing that sends a weight up to hit the bell. After I chopped down on the guy's ankle, I then noticed someone coming at me from my right. I reacted by striking him right in the nose with my glove hand, and it staggered him back. It was Scott Wray, all 6'4" and 220 pounds of him. Before he could recover and rip my brain out of my head, the linesmen got in and pushed me back to the boards, and then my team got in there as well. Not much else happened, but all of Pla-Mors were calling me out. "That was a cheap shot fucker!" "You're fucking dead!" "Dead meat asshole!" and on and on. I was assessed a five-minute major for slashing and a game misconduct, but I wasn't suspended, so I was safe to play the next game. Kevin Carver (our third goalie at the time) finished up. The game ended, and there were no more shenanigans.

The guy that I slashed had a limp for a couple of days, but he was okay. I was glad about that. The only other time I had lost my temper on the ice was when I was 18 and had first started playing. I was playing in a pickup game with some people I knew. This one guy that I didn't know, was being a hot dog, spearing my pads and waving his stick in front of my eyes while the play was going on. I figured I would teach him a lesson. He had the puck on his stick coming in from my right, and I slid out and took his feet out from under him. He cartwheeled and fell into the boards, breaking his elbow. I always felt bad about that. When push comes to shove, we all have to go to work the next day, and no one wants to see anybody get hurt.

Jerry Volsky called me into his office and told me he was thinking of playing Kevin Carver for the second game in Moose Jaw. I assured him I had no problem playing. I wasn't afraid, and I wanted to play. He thought about it for a minute and said ok.

We had to play them a few days later, and I wasn't worried at all. It was on the bus ride that the butterflies started. By game time, it was a full-blown stampede in my stomach, and I considered telling the coach I would rather sit. But the worst thing you can do is show weakness or fear, so I decided to play the game. During warmup, we were skating around, and I got a couple of dirty looks from their players, but nobody said anything. I was fully expecting them to come after me right away. Then the game started and… nothing. Nobody came within ten feet of me. It was the easiest game I played in a long time. We won 6-2 and none of their guys even said a word to me. We shook hands, and everyone went home.

Regina beat Weyburn in two straight games, and the finals were set. We were playing the Blackhawks in a best of three. Coach Volsky called me in to the office. This whole season there had been a kind of disconnect between the coach and the players. I couldn't put my finger on it. On paper, Jerry was the perfect man for the job and was a good communicator. He could be tough as nails when he needed to be, and he knew hockey inside and out, backwards and forwards. But there was just something missing, and all the players felt it. The respect factor just wasn't as high as it should've been. Jerry told me that they had worked out a solution with the league, and Mike Bloski was now eligible to play in the league finals. My heart sank. Mike had played really well while he was in, but I felt my play was almost as good. I told him that I wasn't sure if I was coming back next season, and I would like to play one more home game. He said we would see how

Bloski plays and go from there. I knew I wasn't going to see the ice again, and I wasn't coming back the next year. Chick had such a man crush on Bloski it made me sick. My hockey nobody reputation and lack of resume struck again.

We lost the league final in 3 games. It just seemed like everything came apart at the wrong time. Bloski was heroic in all three games, but it wasn't enough. Watching was painful. The S.A.H.A finals started at the same time. We beat Lumsden, Strasbourg and Esterhazy without losing a game. The finals would be against the Wilkie Outlaws in a 2 out of 3 final. Assiniboia hadn't won a provincial championship in anything in a long time. It was a huge deal. I went to coach Volsky and said that I assumed there was no way I could play that first game at home. He said that he liked it when his players understood his decisions. I understood that I just had to accept my fate, and after this season, there was no way I was ever coming back here. I didn't blame Bloski. He was a great teammate, and he taught me a lot, but I felt completely disrespected.

The first game started, and the two teams were mirror images of each other. It was tightly contested. A great hockey game and our fans went home happy, a 2-1 victory for us. Next game we could win the first provincial championship for Assiniboia in ages.

Wilkie is about 500 km's north of Assiniboia and close to North Battleford. You have to drive through Biggar, (New York is big but this is Biggar), and then you get to Wilkie. Wilkie is a little bit smaller than Assiniboia, about 1,300 people.

We got there about 3 hours before game time and killed a little time before going to the rink. Everyone was pumped up. Just like in our barn, theirs was filled to capacity. The game was a carbon copy of the first game, but this time the

Outlaws came out on top 4-2. We would go back to our barn for the deciding game.

Game 3 would be the talk of the town. Everybody was excited about it. When the game was about to start, the place was again at capacity. The two teams could not be more evenly matched. Unlike the previous two games, we outshot the Outlaws by quite a large margin, but the Wilkie goalie had the game of his life. He made some saves that defied logic. We just could not beat him. The score was tied 1-1 late in the game. The Outlaws got a good chance to score and made the most of it. With just over a minute left, Bloski came to the bench for a sixth attacker. We threw everything at their net. Chili hit the post dead on. The Outlaws picked the puck up and shot the puck the length of the ice into the empty net. Final score 3-1. We lost the league final and the provincial final within a span of 10 days. My senior hockey career came to an end in the most disappointing way possible. I had a knot in my stomach that would last for a week. Losing really sucks.

I had a few days before I had to be back at work so I went around town saying my goodbyes. I told everyone that I wouldn't be back and thanks for everything. For the most part it had been a lot of fun, but the way that it ended left a really sour taste in my mouth. I had heard stories from all the players about times that they had been screwed by the hockey system. Being left off a team because the coach's kid needed the spot. Being blackballed by a league, because one coach who didn't like you spread false rumours. It seemed that every player had a story similar to those, and for the first time in my life, I experienced it. Since I never played minor hockey, I never had to go through the political stuff. Going through it now really sucked.

I went back home, and told my boss that I wouldn't be going back. He was a little sad for me, but that's the way it goes. I was happy to have a job and a boss that had allowed me to go. I returned to work installing paving stones and was actually glad to be there. It was nice to not have any pressure. Not worrying about winning and losing, playing or not playing. Just show up for work and get paid every two weeks. We had this one job installing a driveway for a lady in North Vancouver. She would forever on be known as "The Crazy Lady". She was eccentric to say the least. She would personally inspect every brick that went down. If she deemed a brick to be unsatisfactory in any way, shape or form, she would reject it. And she rejected a lot of them. At least three or four pallets got returned to the supplier, and her driveway only took about ten pallets for the job. A lot of the crew were smokers and it was standard practice to throw the cigarette butts onto the sand and then cover them up with the bricks. If she noticed anybody doing this, she would scream a blood curdling scream. She would then take the bricks up herself until the cigarette butt was exposed, and throw it into a drain on the street. It was actually another crew that was doing this job, but we finished early one day and had time to go and help them. We arrived and were in the carport taking a coffee break when one of the guys on the other crew mentioned that the lady had said that she thought Ken, the foreman on that crew, was "handsome". One of the other guys said that if she thought Ken was handsome, then she was definitely crazy. That's when we heard from the deck above us, "I'M NOT CRAZY".

Chapter 18

Heeeeeeres... Johnny!

After working most of that summer, I was considering my options on where to play for the next season. I heard there was an agent in Calgary who took on almost anybody as a client. His name was Art Breeze and he had connections all over the pro hockey world. I was hoping maybe to go to Europe and play in one of the lower divisions of the pro leagues over there. Or see if it was possible to get some kind of scholarship to a school down in the U.S. I knew that Art Birss had some connections in that area. However, close to the end of August, just as I was going to call him, I got a phone call from Art. The Rebels wanted me back for the next season. With the way the previous season ended, I said not a chance. Art offered me the number one spot and $100 a game, but I wasn't biting. I asked if Komo was coming back. He said that Komo's surgery went really well but that he got an offer to play in England, and he wouldn't be available. I asked about Bloski. As much as I liked Mike, I wasn't about to play second fiddle and sit the entire season. He said Bloski just had shoulder surgery and would be out of action for six months. He said they were trying to find another goalie and hoped to have one before the season started. In the meantime, they would use Kevin Carver. Kevin was a good goalie, but he lived in Regina and wasn't always available. My final question was, "Who was going to coach?" I told him I couldn't play for Jerry Volsky again. There was nothing personal against the guy, because I liked him. He was a good guy and a good coach. But I felt the disrespect I endured, and the disconnect between the coach and players, was too great. Art said that that was not a problem because he was going to assume the coaching duties. Chick wanted to go back to coaching the Bantams, and he couldn't do both jobs. After thinking about it for at least ten seconds, I told Art his terms were acceptable, and that I would be there for the annual Hockey School. I was surprised and happy. I called my boss, and he was happy for me. The dream was still alive.

I arrived in town in September, and I instructed at the hockey school. Komo was there. He had a week before he needed to leave for England. I wouldn't have to handle the kids on my own. The goalie part of the school had expanded from just a few goalies to about 10 or 15, all about the age of 8 or 10. It was an easy task. At that age, all they want to do is stop pucks. They don't want to do skating drills, or learn technical things about the position. They just want to stop shots. So Komo and I came up with all kinds of fun shooting drills and at the end of each session, we split the kids into teams and had a relay race. They loved it. In the last session of the school, they asked that Komo and I race each other. We had to go forward to the end boards, touch them and then skate backwards to the goal line. I was wearing my equipment, and Komo wasn't wearing his. I took off everything I could and made the kids count down 3,2,1, Go! It was a close race, but Komo beat me. I joked with him after that his ass was bigger than mine and was the only reason he won.

The Rebels signed a goalie just before the season started. His name was Dean Ross. He had just finished his junior career playing for the Minot Americans in the Saskatchewan Junior Hockey League. He was 21 and quite the character. He had a cocky attitude but kept it in check. He just had this unshakeable ultra-confidence in his ability. He had an easy way about him, like a guy who just knew he could do anything he wanted, if he put his mind to it. He was a funny guy, and I liked him right away. Which was a good thing, because we rented a house together. Bobby Helland had sold his house, so we rented one on the other side of town. Dean and I would go to the Bar-B and play video games. He was a master and could beat me any time he felt like it. He let me win just enough so that I would keep playing.

Back in the day, when there were six teams in the NIIL, players could get rich playing senior hockey. What would happen is the team would sign a player, pay him, and then get him a job in town that he wouldn't have to show up for. He'd get a regular cheque every two weeks as well as benefits from the company and a cheque once a month from the team. Some players turned down NHL offers because they were making too much money playing senior hockey. But in 1989, senior hockey in Saskatchewan was dying. The economy was such that teams just couldn't afford to pay their players much, if anything. Employment was at a premium, and they couldn't just hand out jobs to transient hockey players, no matter how good they were. The NHL and all the other pro leagues had expanded to the point that there were lots of pro jobs available. Even average players could get a pro tryout somewhere, not to mention the European option.

The South Central Senior Hockey League was disappearing. During the 1989/90 season, the league would consist of only four teams. Regina and Balgonie had dropped out. The Tisdale Ramblers had joined. Tisdale is about 500 kms from Assiniboia and is almost directly north of Regina. We would have some long road trips this season.

For this season, Art recruited Gord Flegel who was another small shifty forward. Gord had played AAA Midget hockey and had participated in the Air Canada Cup Midget tournament when he was 15 or 16. If I'm not mistaken, he was the MVP. He also played 2 years for the Moose Jaw Canucks of the Saskatchewan Junior Hockey League. A notable teammate from that time was Chris Chelios. Gord said that Chelios was the coolest guy he ever met and could talk his way out of any situation. Chelios, during the 1980/81 season, bought two identical cars. Both Vauxhalls. Neither of them ran, so he took the parts from one and added them to the other and got it running. Gord told us that since Chelios was from California, he cut the roof off and drove it like that all winter, a cool guy indeed. After two seasons in Moose Jaw, Gord got a four-year scholarship to Michigan State University. There he played with the likes of Craig Simpson, Bob Essensa, and Norm Foster. He said the atmosphere in their arena was absolutely nuts, and he enjoyed every minute of it. Gord was now living in Moose Jaw and going to the University of Regina to get his Master's degree in teaching. It was one of Art's best recruiting achievements.

We also had a new captain. Paul Tendler was a local guy and a solid player at both ends of the rink. He just exuded leadership. He led by example and did a lot of the dirty work needed to win games. I firmly believe that one should never refer to oneself as a leader. That is a judgement for others to make. Paul commanded respect, and no one ever questioned it. He was our leader and would take us where we wanted to go. We followed his example.

We started the season with some exhibition games. We played two games against Scott Binner's old team from the

Saskatchewan Technical Institute. Close games, but we won both. Dean Ross was sick, so I played both games. Then we played the University of Regina Cougars. We knew this would be a tough game. They had a lot of ex-Regina Pats on the team including their goalie Rod Houk. When I stepped onto the ice for warm-up, I looked down to the other end and thought, "We are going to get killed." All their equipment matched. They had matching helmets, gloves, pants, everything. We had matching jerseys and helmets. Compared to them we looked like rank amateurs, (which we were). I really thought we would get blown out, but it didn't happen. They made the mistake of taking us lightly. They thought they could just show up and win, but we had some good players as well. To a man, nobody wanted to be embarrassed in front of our fans, and we played with a lot of pride. We won 7-3. One of the players on their team, Phil Lepage, was from Gravelbourg. He told us that their coach after the game gave their team a tongue lashing like never before. For their next practice, they had a "bag skate from hell."

We continued to add and subtract players. Darren Lucier was gone, so was Wayne Resch and a few others. The biggest addition for that season was a 6' 3" defenseman named Kevin Tendler. He had played in the Western League with Saskatoon. His draft year was 1979, and he would have been drafted had they still been drafting 20-year old's. He was rated to be drafted first in the second round but around this time was when the NHL switched to drafting 18-year old's, Kevin ended up not getting drafted at all. At first, he said he was devastated. But a day after the draft, he had five NHL offers to choose from. He chose to go to the Washington Capitals. Kevin figured he would have a better chance of making a last place team. He went through the entire exhibition schedule, and in the last game before the regular season started, he scored the tying goal against the defending Champion New York Islanders. He was sent down to the minors the next day and never made it back. He said that he was just having too much fun partying and carousing in the minors to take hockey seriously enough. After a few years, he came back to Saskatchewan and played for Unity before joining us in Assiniboia. Kevin was a great hockey player. When he was on the ice, it was like a giant 15-foot hole in the ice that the opposition would fall into. He was our Ray Bourque. He taught me a lot about how a goalie should interact with his defense. What to say, when to say it, whether they had time or not, how to set up the puck. Some defensemen prefer the puck on their backhand when picking it up behind the net, some on the forehand. He taught me more about goaltending than all the goalies I had played with, and he was a leader, everyone looked up to him.

We also had Brent Castle. Brent is the type of person that takes nothing seriously. In Castle's world, life is one big party, and any situation is an opportunity to make a joke. You could never be in a bad mood with Castle around, he just wouldn't allow it. On top of that, he was built like a fire hydrant. He was 5' 8" tall and about 210 pounds. He seemed to be almost as wide as he was tall, and it was almost impossible to knock him off his skates.

The Rebels had a game in Moose Jaw against the Pla-Mors. I was on the bench in the backup role. The play was breaking out of our end, and Castle received a pass at our blue line and started skating. Everyone who has played full contact hockey knows that you don't look at the puck while you're skating with it. Castle apparently forgot this cardinal rule, because he came full speed, with the puck, with his head down, and was about to skate in front of our bench, (I was at the far end). Kevin Moore was a big defenseman for the

Pla-Mors, 6' 3" and 215 lbs. Moore was a nightmare for most forwards. He was as tough as a two-dollar steak, as mean as a rattlesnake, and he hit like a hammer. He never passed up an opportunity to put somebody through the boards. Moore was an old school defender. Moore saw Castle coming down the wing, with his head down, and I'm sure he licked his chops, knowing he had the opportunity to run Castle into next week. Moore did exactly that. He hit Castle with probably the best body check I have ever seen. Castle hit the boards in front of our bench with such force, he flew head under feet. Literally. His feet were in the twelve o'clock position, and his head was in the six o'clock. To this day, I don't know how I wasn't sliced open. I put my arms up to protect my face, and his skates came down hard and should have sliced through the padding on the underside of my forearms. He landed on his back at my feet with a really loud thud. At the very least, he should've had the wind knocked out of him, instead, he yelled out, CHANGE!! That was Castle.

Our coach, Art Birss had served in the Canadian Army, and he was by far the best motivator I ever played for. He wasn't really into the X's and O's like a lot of modern coaches. We never learned "The Trap" or "The Left-Wing Lock" or any other system you can think of. Art's strategy was a military one. Match up your strengths against their weaknesses, and may the best team win. Basic stuff, and he expected hard work and nothing less than your best effort, all the time. If you took a shift off, you heard about it. Art was very aggressive in his coaching. It went, "Attack! Attack! Attack!" If we were defending, it was, "Get the puck back so we can attack again!" A lot of times, Art would pick out the opposition's weakest defender, and when that guy was on the ice, he would have us dump the puck into his corner and overwhelm him with numbers. Sometimes, all 3 forwards would be on this one defenseman, trying to get the puck. Art wasn't going to let the other team's best players beat us. He wanted their worst players to have to play to a level that matched ours. He always wanted our intensity level at its highest, and if fights broke out, he was ok with that, as long as we won those too. Art was a no- nonsense coach when it came to game time, but after the game, he was loose and a jokester. One guy told me that after a game he went into the shower and as he was washing his hair and face, Art had come in next to him. The guy said that after he got all the soap out of his eyes, he looked over, and Art was pissing on his leg and laughing.

We had a young player on our team, (I forget his name), and he was willing to do just about anything to stay in the lineup. One game, he took it upon himself to fight one of the other team's tougher guys. The fight was pretty even to begin with, and both guys got some good shots in. But our guy was overmatched and, in the end, took a pretty good beating. Between periods, Art went up to this kid and said, "Not bad." The kid said, "Thanks coach," and then Art said, "I think you should fight him again while his hands are still sore."

On Dec. 9th, 1989, The Rebels played a game at home. After the game, we all went to Bar-B. The next day would be my 28th birthday, and I had been playing ice hockey for exactly 10 years. Since it was already 11:00 p.m. by the time we got to the bar, everybody decided it would be close enough for me to celebrate. When I arrived, I noticed that they had put up a huge banner that read, 'HAPPY BIRTHDAY JERRY.' The girls who worked in the bar made a cake for me. It was the shape of a rectangle and decorated to look like a hockey rink. At one end was a net with about a hundred pucks in it. It was hilarious, and I was honoured that someone would do that for me. I sat down with a few people I knew and was waiting for the waitress to come over so I could order a drink.

Before she appeared, this guy that I barely knew came up to me and offered to buy me one. I told him that I would like a Paralyzer. Back in 1989, this was a five-dollar drink and the most expensive one on the menu. When Chili would order one, he would say, "I'll have a Paralyzer, and hope it doesn't work." After a few minutes, the waitress brought me the drink and put it on the table. Within about ten minutes, our table was covered in Paralyzers. Everybody in the bar it seemed, wanted to buy me a drink. I did my best to drink them all, but after about the fifth one I was so full of milk, I couldn't take another sip. It was one of the only times that I drank so much, I forgot some of the things I did. I tried as hard as I could not to throw up, but it was a losing battle. Several times I did the technicolor yawn outside in the parking lot. Over the next couple of days, I had people approach me and tell me how funny I had been, and then describe the things that I had no memory of. Apparently, I went a little overboard getting birthday kisses from all the girls. Terrie was not pleased.

At Christmas that year Dean had bought the book "Home Game: Hockey Life in Canada", by Ken Dryden as a present for his older brother. We had found out that Mr. Dryden was going to be in Regina for a book signing for one afternoon. His brother was a big Montreal Canadiens fan so it was only natural that we head up to Regina that day and get the book autographed. We got to the shopping mall where the event was to take place and got in line. I mentioned that his brother was a big fan of the Canadiens, but this one guy standing half a dozen people ahead of us was, what I believe to be, the biggest Montreal Canadiens fan I have ever encountered. The guy was decked out in all Montreal Canadiens apparel. His hat, jersey, jacket, sweatpants, running shoes, socks, and even his shoelaces were festooned with the Canadiens logo. I am positive that had we pulled his sweatpants down that even his underwear would be decorated this way. Mr Dryden came and was seated at a table with a line of about 250 people all the way down the mall. The big Montreal fan got to the table and Mr. Dryden signed his book, shook the guys hand and had a short conversation with him. It took about another ten minutes for us to get to the front of the line. I was never one to collect autographs or go gaga over celebrities. It was cool to meet him, having watched him play in 1971, but I never said a word. Dean asked him to autograph it for his brother and said "Thank you Mr. Dryden", and we walked away. We were looking at the autograph as we were walking to the exit when we came across the guy with all the Habs gear. He was holding a girl that had stood in line with him, and he was sobbing. Tears were just rolling down his cheeks. The guy was literally weeping. Dean and I just looked at each other in amazement. Being a fan is one thing, but to take it to that level, to me, shows mental instability. I truly hope that guy got some help.

The schedule for this season had become almost monotonous as our games were against the same three teams all year, Tisdale, Weyburn, Moose Jaw. There was the odd exhibition game thrown into the mix. You just got sick of playing the same teams over and over again. We couldn't wait to get to the end of the season so we could play in the S.A.H.A playdowns and see somebody different. The S.A.H.A. playoffs started in late January, and we had to play Yellow Grass. Yellow Grass is the smallest town we had played in since I had joined the Rebels. Population 300. Future NHLer Peter Schaefer (who would play for my Canucks) was from Yellow Grass. Schafer would've been about 12 at this time and probably watched the game. When we went out for warm-up, we noticed that the rink was not regulation size. It was probably 20% smaller than our rink. There wouldn't be much room to maneuver. I was starting and Dean Ross was the backup. I went in and took my warmup shots, and then Dean went in for his. The third shot after I had left the net, Kent Blythe let go a rocket from the faceoff dot and nailed Dean right in the forehead. I can still hear the sound it made. I had to count my lucky stars I had gotten out when I did. Dean was flat on his back, spread eagle like he was going to do snow angels. The training staff ran out to him and after a few minutes got him sitting up. You could almost see the birds flying around his head. He took a few more minutes and said he was fine, then went and sat on the bench to gather himself. Kent didn't have the hardest shot in the world, but it was decent. This was in the days before composite sticks. If Kent had been using one of those, Dean probably would've woken up in the hospital.

Yellow Grass was close to Weyburn, so they had mostly Weyburn's players. They didn't add anybody so the outcome was a foregone conclusion. We had added a couple of really good players. We were up 4-0 in the third period when Brad Varga got a questionable major penalty. They scored three goals on the power play, but that was as close as they would get. Final score 4-3. The second game was played in our arena and we won 8-3.

Dean had always wanted to be a police officer, like his older brother and had been accepted to the academy in Regina. He had to leave the team with a big lump on his forehead. My most vivid memory of Dean is when we drove to Regina together to visit his parents and pick up a few things. He showed me a picture that gives me goosebumps to this day when I think about it. Dean had played a few games for the Prince Albert Raiders in the Western League in 1986. One of those games was against the Swift Current Broncos. In the picture, Dean is in goal and there are four Swift Current players all around him. The four players in the picture were the ones that were killed in a bus crash on Dec. 30th of that year.

R.I.P

Trent Kresse
Scott Kruger
Chris Mantyka
Brent Ruff

The next practice after Dean left, much to my surprise, in walks Mike Bloski. His shoulder had healed enough for him to play, but he was out of shape. Art came to me and said that they really had no choice. They had to sign a goalie, and Mike was available. Art assured me that it would not be a repeat of last season. I had earned my spot, and Mike would not replace me. I knew Art was as good as his word so I welcomed Mike back with open arms.

We still had some regular season games left to play. Mike started a game in late January against Moose Jaw. I noticed that he had new gloves. He explained that his younger brother was playing junior in North Battleford, and that the team had given him new gloves so he sent his old ones to Mike. Mike called them "hand-me-ups." Mike played the first two periods, and you could see the rust. I had to play the third period because his shoulder was getting sore, but we won easily. Mike and I pretty much split the games the rest of the way.

We breezed through the next two rounds of S.A.H.A opponents and beat Moose Jaw in the first round of league playoffs. We were in the final of both the league playoffs and S.A.H.A. Mike and I alternated games, and it was working out better than I could've hoped. Mike and I had such differing styles that it really affected the other teams. Mike's style of goaltending was more instinctual than technical, much like mine but in a different way. He had that way of making players shoot the puck right at him. I tried to copy it in practice, but it never worked for me. Guys would end up just going around me and putting the puck into the open net. Mike couldn't really teach me anything about the physical side of goaltending. He taught me more about the mental aspect. How to stay focused. How to be mentally strong. The best thing he taught me was the "ten second rule." The "ten second rule" was that, after letting in a goal, give yourself ten seconds to hate yourself for failing, then forgive yourself. Wash it away like a stain. He told me that the most important save you're ever going to make is the next one. And that in the big picture, the win is the most important thing. Doesn't matter if they score 20 on you, if your team scores 21, it's a win. Always think of the big picture. I used the "ten second rule" for the rest of my career. It always gave me a sense of peace. A goal was never going to be a case of life and death and wasn't worth stressing about. The next save was what mattered. The best asset any goalie can have is a short memory.

The league final would be played against Tisdale, and the provincial final would be against Eston. Both teams coincidentally, were called the Ramblers. Tisdale finished ahead of us in the standings at the end of the season, so to save money, the league final would have game 1 in our barn, and game 2 and game 3 (if necessary) would be played in Tisdale. Tisdale came to our arena for game 1 of the final, and we won that game 8-3. Eston came a few nights later, and we won that one. So, we were up 1 game to none in both series. As it turned out, we had to play Friday night in Eston and Saturday in Tisdale, a distance of almost 500 kms and a 7-hour bus ride.

CHAPTER 19

Reversal of Fortune

Friday night we get to Eston. Eston is in Western Saskatchewan and has a population of about 1,100 people, and their rink was about 40 years old. There was chicken wire at each end, and there were about 3 rows of bench type stands that held maybe 200. We got onto the ice, and I could not believe my eyes. There was nothing protecting the fans in the bleachers from flying pucks, and the bleachers were full. The first row of fans had their feet on top of the boards. When we were skating around for the pregame, a couple of players got spit on. When you got hit into the boards, the fans could literally grab you and pull you into the stands, if they were so inclined. The other side of the rink where the benches were, was standing room only, and again, nothing keeping them from reaching over the boards and grabbing a player or a referee. In my book, it was a real safety concern. They had about 500 or so people jammed into that arena, and it was pandemonium. The game started, and Mike was in net. We really wanted to take care of business and not have to worry about a Game 3, but the Eston team had different plans. It was a close game with Eston leading after two periods 4-3. The third period had been our best all year, but it wasn't to be this game. Eston scored three more times to go up 7-3. We scored one late, but by then, it didn't matter. We would have to play Game 3 in our arena the following Saturday night. We had to get changed, showered and get out of there in a hurry, because we had a long bus ride ahead of us. For some reason, and I will forever wonder what the guys were thinking, we stopped at the bar to buy booze on the way out of town. I would think that the guys would take it easy and have a beer or two on the ride, but hockey players are not known for their discretion. About half the guys got absolutely hammered. We arrived in Tisdale at about 5:30 in the morning. A few of the Tisdale players were still up and met the bus just outside of town. A lot of the players knew each other from previous teams. After a short conversation, we got to the motel. This is where Tisdale played a little dirty pool. They put us up in the worst dive in town. The rooms were freezing. There were gaps at the bottom of the doors where snow and wind would come in. You had to put a rolled-up towel down, but that really didn't help a lot.

In the motel hallway, Art called me over to his room Saturday afternoon. I was half expecting him to say that Mike would be starting tonight, but that wasn't it. Not this time. He knew that we would be in tough that night and that I would need to be at my best. Art, the big-time motivator had told me, "The guys are tired from playing last night. On the long bus ride, half of them got gooned on the trip over and are hungover to the nines. I'll make you a deal. If you win this game for us, you can play Saturday against Eston." Art was the master. He knew just what button to push with me. He knew how bitter I was about the previous season. I smiled like the Cheshire Cat and said, "I will see you on the bus tonight, with the trophy."

Saturday Night came, the game started, and we were horrible. I was back to feeling like I was playing in a blender.

They were all over us. I made a lot of saves, but it was 4-0 before we finally scored a goal. We managed to score another before the end of the first and entered the second period down 4-2. The second period was more of the same. We would close the gap, and they would pull further ahead. One play really sticks out in my head about that game. Darcy Simoneau was a talented player and scored a lot of goals, but he always had a screw loose. On this particular play, a shot came at me from well out, I went to my knees and stopped the shot. The puck hit my stick at a funny angle and popped up right in front of me. Darcy was standing next to the crease and grabbed his stick like a baseball bat and swung as hard as he could and completely missed the puck. He struck me directly across the chest. I felt the blow but it didn't hurt (much). I have a theory that I put to good use most of the time. When someone cheap shots you, show no reaction. It will affect them more if you act like nothing happened. After Darcy's home run attempt, the puck fell harmlessly into my glove. I stood up and looked at him and said, "Hey Darce." He just looked at me and said, "Fuck!" and skated away.

The second period ended with Tisdale ahead 7-4. Like I said before, the third period had been our friend all season. I knew that I had kept the team within striking distance and hoped it was enough. The third period started, and Tisdale seemed to be content to sit on the lead. Always a dangerous strategy. About halfway through the period, I thought to myself, "We need an explosion." Just then, the P.A. announcer came over the speakers and said, "Tomorrow's game will be held at 2:00 p.m. right here at Tisdale Arena. If you need tickets, see any member of the executive committee. Next game, 2:00 p.m. here at Tisdale Arena." What a colossal blunder. I wonder if the guy who made that announcement still has nightmares about it. We scored about 10 seconds later. 2 minutes and 13 seconds after that, we had a two-goal lead. While we were still one behind, Kevin Tendler had the puck about 10 feet inside the blue line. He wound up for a slapshot and Gil Hudon, the Tisdale goalie, came out aggressively and challenged him. Instead of shooting, K.T. made a slap pass to Chili, who was standing all alone behind and beside the goalie. Chili got the puck and had all day to shoot it in the wide-open net. He put it in off the post. Asshole. He said after the game that he was still hung over and was seeing double. Thank God it went in. Anyway, we were up 9-7 and coming down the stretch. 2 minutes left and Tisdale is coming on strong. I made some saves, and the defense did the rest. We scored an empty net goal with less than a minute to go. League Champions!! What a comeback! What a game! Everybody came rushing at me, but I dodged them. Howard and Art were running out onto the ice. I skated over to them and hugged them both. I then shouted, "I get to play…Saturday!!" and they both laughed.

The bus ride home was a party like I have never seen. We were so happy that we didn't have to stay in our freezing motel rooms another night. We stopped at the bar and got booze, a lot of booze. We were in no danger of running out, and we probably could've filled the bus gas tank. I still have pictures of that bus ride home. People are soaked, clothes are torn, and a couple of people are passed out. It was a six-hour ride of pure party time. The league trophy was just that, a trophy. It was not a cup. Someone had snuck a beer glass out of the bar, and we taped it to the top of the trophy, so we could drink out of it. You can't celebrate a championship if you can't drink out of the trophy! We arrived back in town at about five in the morning. Some of our fans greeted us at the rink. Everybody somehow poured themselves out of the bus without injury, and we all got rides home from the fans who had shown up at the rink. We had one championship down but still a lot of work to do. It was nice to celebrate, but the big challenge was still ahead of us.

That week we practiced a couple of times. The guys were amped up like never before. I was hoping that we hadn't peaked too soon. The game Saturday was the talk of the town. Nobody wanted to talk about anything else, and it turned out to be a long week.

Saturday finally came, and the air was filled with electricity. I was super nervous, which isn't like me. We went out for warm up, and the arena is jam packed. Like I said before, the arena seats 914 people. They had almost 1,500 jammed in there. I don't know how the fire-marshal had allowed it. A couple of hundred Eston fans had made the trip, and one of them had the loudest horn I have ever heard. It was like a train was going by. Two players on the Eston team were from Ponteix, which is about an hour west of Assiniboia. It's a town of about 500. A hundred of them made the trip to see their boys play. I couldn't shake the butterflies. Like Leo Cahill used to say on the CFL broadcasts, "I was more nervous than a long-tailed cat in a room full of rocking chairs." The atmosphere and the expectations were so high that all I could think about was failure. The game was also being broadcast on the radio. They brought a play by play guy in from some junior team, and Howard Mehain was the colour commentator. The game finally started, and it was like both teams were shot out of a cannon. I still couldn't shake my nerves. My body was not doing what I wanted it to do. My legs felt like jelly. The crowd was so loud that you couldn't hear the whistle. Eston scored first, but it wasn't a good goal. It was a fairly weak shot that trickled through my legs. Fuck. The first period ended with Eston up 1-0. I made a few saves, but I really didn't like how I was feeling. Hopefully the break would help me calm my nerves. Nope. The second period started, and Eston scored to go up 2-0. Again, not a great goal. It was at this point I said to myself, "Fucking forget who's watching and play the fucking game." It was like a piano had been lifted off my shoulders. I started playing with confidence, and I was calm and cool but intense. The zone. Shortly after, they got a breakaway. A guy named Jerry Bick (no relation) got a pass behind our defense at our blue line. He was a left-handed shot, coming at me from my right. I had him pegged for a shot high to my glove side, so I cheated slightly that way. So much for my clairvoyance, he faked the shot and deked to my right. I was caught flat footed and kind of half dove and half laid down to my right. Realizing that he had the whole net to shoot at, I flipped over onto my back and ala Dominik Hasek, lifted my legs straight up, Mr. Bick, (still no relation), shot the puck directly into my pads. Howard told me afterward that the play by play guy went nuts, "BIG SAVE HACK!!! I CAN'T BELIEVE WHAT I JUST SAW!!" Not long after, Scott Binner scored to cut the lead in half. We went to the dressing room down 2-1. The third period is our friend I kept telling myself. The Eston team made the same mistake as the Tisdale team. They tried to sit on the lead and nurse it home. About halfway through the period, another explosion happened. This time three goals in about a two and a half- minute span. With ten minutes to go, we were ahead by two. About two minutes later, Eston got a shot from the point. I stopped it and tried to steer it to the corner. I misjudged slightly, and it went right to another Eston player standing in the faceoff circle. He one timed a shot that I just missed with my blocker, and the score was 4-3. 8 minutes to go. We didn't sit back. Art with his attacking style made sure we kept the pressure on them. They never really got another chance, and with less than a minute to go, we got an empty netter to salt the game away. Provincial Champions!! It was absolute pandemonium in that arena. Three short years ago, the Rebels couldn't even come close to winning a game. Now we were league and provincial champions! All the extreme disappointment of the previous year made this championship season all that much sweeter. It was sheer jubilation, and I had never been so happy. We took our victory lap with the Henderson Cup, symbolic of the Saskatchewan Senior A Championship. Years later, people of the town were still saying that it was the best game ever played in that arena.

We celebrated in the dressing room. Mike Bloski was so happy for me, he came and sat on my lap and rubbed my head like a proud papa. I have a picture of it. As we were all getting undressed, Bloski called everyone back out onto the ice so we could get a team picture with the cup, just like the Edmonton Oilers. Some people were nearly naked, but we all went out and posed for the picture. We were expected at the Franklin Hotel for a celebration, as they had taken over sponsorship of the team, and we had to get there. Everybody got dressed and headed over. Brent Castle had gone to ten provincial finals in a row and lost every time, and me being the longest serving Rebel, the two of us got to bring the cup into the bar. Tim Nickel was actually the longest serving Rebel, but being a Christian, he didn't go to the bar. It seemed like a thousand people were in there, and when we opened the door, the cheer was deafening. We put the Henderson Cup on the counter and continued to celebrate. After the bar closed down, one of the farmers from just outside of town bravely offered his house for a party. I think everyone in town was there. I have a picture of me and Art arm in arm, drunk as skunks. Art will forever be my hero. He believed in me when others only saw a hockey nobody.

Chapter 20
Domination

The 1990/91 season would see even more changes. The South Central Senior Hockey League had folded. The Rebels were trying desperately to help form a "Super-League" where all Senior A teams in Saskatchewan would play in one league. Too many teams had opted out because of high costs, so the Rebels were left scrambling. The only league they could find was the Yellowhead Hockey League. It would mean a lot of travel as all the teams would be north of Regina. The league would consist of six teams: Assiniboia, Kamsack, Tisdale, Canora, Esterhazy and Bredenbury. At least we wouldn't have to play the same teams over and over again. Well, that's what I thought until I learned that Tisdale, Bredenbury, and Kamsack had all dropped out. Leaving a three-team league. It was going to be even worse than last year, and our team was going to be even stronger. We added Jim Misener, Cliff Mapes, Scott Wray, (who I once punched in the face, and was still expecting payback), and defenseman Kevin Moore from Moose Jaw, and Phil Lepage from Gravelbourg who had played for the Regina Pats, and the University of Regina. My goaltending partner was going to be Rob Grainger who was a local guy and was the best goalie in the Noteku, (Pronounced NOT-a-cue), Hockey League, a Senior B league. At this time,

Mike Bloski had gone to Whitehorse to play. We had a lot of great players. I didn't see how we were going to lose a game this season.

The first half of the season, we were a bit inconsistent. We had guys injured and others in and out of the lineup. Rob Grainger played some good games, but ultimately it was just a little bit above his ability level. But we still won way more than we lost. After Christmas, the rich got richer. Mr. Grainger was sent back down to the Noteku league, and my buddy Komo returned to the fold. I couldn't have been happier. His time in England had been a little frustrating. Because of the import rule, he wasn't allowed to play in league games. Only exhibition, and there weren't that many of those. He said that one rink they played in had one square corner. The door where the ice cleaning machine came in and out was squared off. Funny. He could only coach, and he said the goalies were terrible. In January, with Komo back in the lineup and our roster intact, we started playing more consistently. The other two teams in the league were pretty evenly matched with each other, but we were head and shoulders better than them. The only time we would lose a game, was when we became overconfident.

In February, we made a return to Alaska and this time with a much better team. We didn't travel to Whitehorse this time, so I wouldn't get to visit Mike Bloski. We travelled by bus to Calgary and then flew to Vancouver, Seattle, Anchorage, and finally, Fairbanks. Since we were going to have to leave right after the game on Saturday, Komo and I decided to flip a coin for who would start the Friday night game; knowing that the team would be hungover as hell for the Saturday game. Komo won the toss and got the Friday game. I would be fed to the wolves on Saturday. Komo and I decided to go out with the rest of the guys and party hard. If everyone else was going to party, then we weren't going to be left out. The Friday game was an even-steven affair, but the Gold Kings came out on top 6-4 with an empty net goal. Komo got the usual, "HEY GOALIE, WHAT'S THE SCORE!?" routine. I didn't drink a whole lot, but more than I normally would have the night before a game. We closed down the bar at 5:00am in the morning. I managed to sleep until about 11:00, but that was it. There was just too much activity in the hotel to be able to sleep any longer. I was tired and a little bit hungover. I got something to eat and went out shopping with a few of the other guys. We were all wearing our team sweatsuits and made quite an impression on some of the young kids who were shopping with their parents. They kept dropping their jaws and pointing at us. Funny. In the afternoon, I tried to get a nap in, but it was a no go. I had my pregame meal with the team and prepared for the inevitable beatdown we were about to get. Some of the guys were egregiously hungover. Sometimes, all common sense goes out the window when you're on the road. When game time came, I started to feel a little bit better. I seemed to have quite a bit of energy. I try not to look into the stands when I play because it's too much of a distraction. But, in warmup there was this girl in a white dress up to my right. She really stood out, and I couldn't stop looking up in her direction. I thought to myself, "I had better get my head straight, or this could be really embarrassing, but damn that girl is good looking." The game started, and I couldn't have been more wrong about it getting embarrassing. I was stopping everything, and I felt great. I don't know how a hummingbird sees things. I'm pretty sure everything to them is in slow motion. That's how I felt. Like everything was going half speed except me. I was moving faster than everyone else. I stopped 20 shots in the first period, a lot of quality saves, and we were up 3-0. The second period went almost the same, another 20 saves for me and another goal for us. 4-0. The third period came and you could sense the frustration coming from the other team and their fans. About halfway through the period, they finally got one behind me, and then about 30 seconds later, another one. But I wasn't the least bit concerned. We were still two up with less than half a period to go, and I was still feeling great. One of their players blasted a slapshot at me from about 15 feet. It was along the ice, and I just calmly went into the butterfly and angled my stick slightly, and the shot hit my stick and deflected to the glass in the corner of the rink just above the boards. All the fans in that corner hit the deck. I had to laugh. It was the weirdest feeling in the world. I just knew that no one was going to score on me. It was almost serene-like. In the final minute, the Gold Kings pulled their goalie, and we scored an empty net goal. After the goal and assists were announced over the P.A., our whole bench stood up and yelled, "HEY GOALIE, WHAT'S THE SCORE? 1, 2, 3, 4, 5, YEAAAAAAAHHHHHH!" Well the Alaska fans didn't take too kindly to that. Garbage, pop cans, beer cans, plastic cups, programs, and anything else they could get their hands on rained down onto our bench. We didn't care though because we had just won. In the end, I stopped 56 out of 58 shots. Just one of those nights where you can do no wrong. We had a mini celebration in the dressing room, but we had to get to the airport. It really was a shame that we couldn't stay and party one more night, but that's life. I continued to feel really good until we got to the airport. Then my bubble burst, and I could hardly stay awake. On the many plane rides home, I woke up periodically and everyone would be staring at me with these shit eating grins on their faces. I had no idea what they were doing to me, but I couldn't stay awake if my life depended on it. It turned out that they were just messing with my head. They hadn't done anything.

The rest of the season was anticlimactic. We had such a good team, there really wasn't anyone who could touch us. We won the league title easily, and the provincial title wasn't much harder. It was still a big deal but didn't have the impact of the previous year. I didn't know it at the time, but the last provincial playoff game would be my last in a Rebel uniform.

CHAPTER 21

California Dreamin'

In the summer of 1991, Art Birss left Assiniboia for Whitehorse. He had been hired to coach the Whitehorse Huskies in the newly formed Pacific Northwest Senior Hockey League. That league would have a total of six teams: The Huskies, Anchorage Aces, Fairbanks Gold Kings, Abbotsford Flyers, Stony Plain (Alberta) Eagles, and the Assiniboia Southern Rebels. I, on the other hand, was headed in the other direction. I felt I had nothing left to accomplish in Assiniboia, and I wanted to see if I could get a tryout in the East Coast League. Scotty Binner had gotten one in Dayton, Ohio. Art, in his last act as GM of the Rebels had gotten me a tryout with a semi-pro team in Fresno, California called the Fresno Falcons. In anticipation of this tryout, I played as much as I could over the summer, maybe a dozen times, and I sucked every time. I just could not get it together. Darryl Lauer, the coach and GM of the Falcons was coming up to Vancouver at the end of August to try out a bunch of players. Art had told him about me, and I had talked to Darryl on the phone a couple of times. He had no idea who I was, (of course), and was taking Art at his word that I would be an asset to his team. It concerned me that I wasn't playing very well. My body just would not do what I wanted, and I was getting frustrated. I had played through slumps before, but this was worse. It was like I had lost my ability to play. The harder I tried, the worse it got. I could only hope I could work it out before the tryout came. I didn't. I got to the rink the day of the tryout. There were about 30 guys there, but only one other goalie. Not everybody was trying out, some were there for free ice time. When the tryout started, we did some drills, and I did ok. Once the scrimmage started though, I couldn't stop a thing. Guys were scoring on me from everywhere. I couldn't have stopped a curling rock if it was sliding towards me. I felt like it was my first time playing. One shot was going wide, and I reached out with my stick and deflected it into my own net. It couldn't have gone any worse. I got dressed and left the rink without showering. I briefly spoke to Darryl, apologized for wasting his time and drove home. I never expected to hear from him and was going to phone Frank Hamel to see if it wasn't too late to come back to Assiniboia for my 5th season. Before I could, the phone rang. It was Darryl, and he had spoken to Art and told him about the tryout. Art had assured him that I was a quality goalie, and I had just had a bad day. Darryl said again that he was taking Art at his word, and that he was leaving for California the next day and I could ride with him if I wanted. I said, "Hell yeah," and hoped that my slump would end on the way to California.

When we arrived in Fresno, it was 106°F. I had never felt heat like that. You couldn't be outside for more than a few minutes. The first couple of nights, I stayed at Darryl's house. He had arranged a furnished apartment for me and a roommate, but it wouldn't be ready for another couple of days. Darryl lived in a huge rancher with his sister Pat. It had a pool in the backyard, and I put that to good use.

There was about 6 weeks before the start of the season, and Darryl had arranged a job for me on a construction site with one of the other players. His name was Al, and he was from Ontario. The construction site was in a part of town where they were building a whole subdivision. About 30 houses were being built all at once. There was a small park in the center of the subdivision, and in this park was a huge pile of garbage. Everything from drywall and two by fours to any kind of construction material you could think of. The pile was at least 15 feet high and just as wide and about 30 yards long. Our job was to fill a pickup truck with material from the pile and take it to a garbage bin that they had delivered, about 100 yards away. We could only work in the mornings until it got to about 95 degrees. The boss just told us that when it got too hot, find a house where nobody was working and hide out. If he needed us for something, he would find us. It wouldn't be too hard. The pickup truck would be right outside. It took Al and me about a week to get rid of the pile, and the boss was tickled pink. He had said that they hired a lot of hockey players over the years, and the great majority of them were dogfuckers. It would've taken them a year to get rid of that pile. Al and I didn't even think we were working that hard. We spent most of the day just talking and joking. Al was an out of work teacher, and he would tell me stories of things that his students tried to get away with. He was only there because he wasn't able to get a job for that school year.

During this time, I met my roommate Alan Miller. He was from Michigan and was a huge Wolverines and Detroit Red Wings fan. He was a smoker, but he didn't smoke in the apartment so that was huge. He was a super funny guy and could do impressions. He would mimic my laugh, which would only make me laugh harder. He could do Homer Simpson to a tee, and a bunch of others too. We got along really well. We had another roommate move in, but there were only two bedrooms. Leo, the new guy, would have to sleep on the couch. Rent was reduced by a third, which helped out immensely. Living was cheap in California. You could get a whole shopping cart full of food for next to nothing.

Before Leo came along, Alan and I were short on money. My first payday was a few days away, and Alan came up with a way to get some cash. He had a collection of trading cards that was worth a lot of money. He had a Roberto Clemente rookie card, which these days can be worth up to $40,000, I don't know what it was worth in 1991, but it was a lot. He also had a Nolan Ryan rookie card, which in today's market can be worth $25,000. He had a bunch of Steve Yzerman rookie cards, as well as Jose Cansecos and a whole bunch of others. It was an impressive collection. We went to this small sporting collectibles store and talked to the guy behind the counter. He was obviously the owner. Miller put his binder on the counter and opened it and told the guy that he wanted to sell a few of his cards. The guy started browsing through it while we stood there. When he finished looking through the whole collection, he closed the binder and gave a big sigh and spoke like he was doing Miller a huge favour, "I'll give you $300 for the whole thing." I don't know how Miller kept his composure. The collection wasn't even mine, and I couldn't have been more insulted. I wanted to jump over the counter and slap the guy. But Miller just kind of chuckled and told him he wasn't interested in selling the whole thing, just enough of the cards to get some cash, and then, only ones that he had duplicates of. Miller and the guy negotiated, and Miller sold a few of his cards for $60. After we left Miller, said to me, "That guy thinks I'm a fuckin' idiot," and I told Miller that I agreed with that guy. He laughed. Miller and I went to a bar one night with some of the other guys on the team, a band started playing and they opened up the dance floor by moving some tables. Miller asked a girl at the table next to us if she wanted to dance. The lady politely declined. Miller got up and said "that's ok, I gotta go take a shit anyway."

When time came for training camp, I was really hoping that my slump was over. We got to the practice rink which was the only rink I have ever been in where the dressing rooms are outside. You had to dress in 100°F weather and then walk into the rink where it's 25°F. It was quite the contradiction, and I hated it. By the time I was dressed, I was drenched in sweat which would then freeze to me. It was awful. Luckily this was not the rink we would play our home games at. Fresno actually had a really nice arena. My first day at training camp was better than my tryout. I was actually able to make some saves, but it wasn't that many. My body still felt like it was a foreign entity and would just not do what I was asking it to do. There were 3 other goalies. One was Canadian, his name was Shannon, and he said that he had played for the Victoria Cougars. I kind of doubted it. He just wasn't that good. The other goalies were local guys.

After that first day of camp, Darryl addressed the team. The expansion San Jose Sharks and the Los Angeles Kings were going to have an exhibition game in Fresno, and we were expected to work at the game. I wasn't sure what he meant. As far as I knew, every arena had their own staff and me being a foreigner, I wasn't legally allowed to work in the States. Even my construction job was paid under the table. He said that only the locals would be working. Anyone from outside the country would just be hanging around, acting as gophers or helping out anywhere they could. This was cool. I was hoping that maybe I would get to meet Kelly Hrudey.

Also, at this time, the 1991 Canada Cup was going on. Hockey wasn't huge in Fresno and only one bar in town was showing the final game between Canada and the United States. Canada had won the first game, and this game might decide the Championship. Miller, a few of the other guys and I went to the bar to watch the game and set up a row of chairs right in front of the big screen tv, about 10 or 12 feet back. Almost nobody was there when we arrived. The game went on and the waitress brought us our drinks. I never went to the bathroom during the game so I had no reason to turn around. I was dimly aware that other people had entered the bar and sat behind us, but I didn't think much of it, and I was glued to the tv. When the game was over, I stood up to go to the bathroom, and the Los Angeles Kings were sitting about 10 feet behind us. Kelly Hrudey wasn't there, but I recognized Larry Robinson, Rob Blake, Luc Robitaille, Marty McSorley, Steve Weeks, as well as a few others, and tough guy Jay Miller. They all got up to leave as Wayne Gretzky (who hadn't played because in a previous game, he had suffered a back injury) lifted up the Canada Cup. Jay Miller said, "Hmph, doesn't look too hurt." I think his career ended shortly thereafter.

The next night was the exhibition game. Since I wasn't working, I sat in the stands and got to watch for free. Kelly Hrudey wasn't playing, in fact, not many of the regulars were. I only recognized a few names on each team. David Goverde, who I had never heard of, played goal for the Kings, and Jarmo Myllys, who I was barely aware of, was the Sharks goalie. I don't remember much about the game, but it was pretty boring. I remember Myllys shooting the puck about 60 feet in the air from his goal line to just outside his own blueline and saying to myself, "I'd like to be able to do that." Other than that, nothing about the game stands out. We were practicing right after the NHL game was over, so I wanted to get out onto the ice as quickly as I could. It was about a sixty-yard walk from the dressing room to the rink. I passed the medical room and saw Jeff Madill, who had played for San Jose that night, getting treatment for his shoulder. I only looked at him for maybe two seconds as I passed by the doorway, but he looked at me like I had just killed his dog. As I was about to go on the ice, I looked to my right and there stood Kelly Hrudey. I've never been an autograph hound, but I would've walked up to him to shake his hand and say hello, but he was standing in the area where the ice cleaning machine went in and out of the building and it was concrete. I just gave him a nod and stepped onto the ice. I didn't wait to see if he nodded back. I have no doubt in my mind that if I saw him today, he would remember me. Maybe not.

The practice went fairly well. I seemed to be getting control of my body back, but it was still a struggle. There were six goalies in camp now, and I was head and shoulders better than all of them (my humble expert opinion), but I just couldn't prove it. Watching them all, I couldn't help but think they were all average. Shannon was the best of the bunch, and he was barely above average from what I could tell. This went on for about another two weeks when I got a phone call. It was Art Birss calling from Whitehorse. He asked me how it was going. I told him it could be better. He said, "Well, I'm sending you a plane ticket. We're playing the Russians!" He said that Bloski, (who had played in Whitehorse the previous season), hurt his knee and that he was retiring. They needed another goalie, and I was first on his list. He said that the Huskies didn't pay their players but guaranteed me a spot on the team, a job and a place to live. I said that I hated not finishing what I started, but the Falcons had offered me no guarantees, I wasn't even sure I'd be on the team when the season started, so I agreed to his terms and waited for the plane ticket to arrive. The flight wasn't until almost a week later, so I worked at the construction site for a few more days. The boss seemed genuinely upset that I was leaving. Big Al, my partner at the job site, had left earlier. He had unexpectedly received a job offer at a private school in Ontario. Too bad, he was the best player on the team. The boss said he was going to miss me because the two or three other players he had hired were dog-fuckers. The boss told me that his boss had said about one of the guys, "If I see that fucker leaning on his shovel one more time, he's gone!" He was talking about Shannon. The day before the flight, the last Falcon's practice that I would attend took place. I just watched. I didn't want to take a chance on getting injured. Afterward, I said my goodbyes. With a few exceptions, I liked the guys. They had been good to me. A few of them said, "You're leaving? What the fuck?" I told them that Darryl had traded me to Whitehorse for a bunch of pucks and some tape. Darryl said that it better be black tape or the deal was off. That was the end of my California adventure. I felt strange. I had never quit a team before, and I really did want to finish what I had started. I figured that if Whitehorse didn't work out, maybe I could come back. The next day, I took a bus from Fresno to San Francisco. This huge African American guy, who looked like he was having a really bad day, sat next to me. He must've been 6' 4" tall and 325 pounds, but solid, not fat. I didn't say a word. He looked like he could snap me in two without much effort. For the whole four hours we sat together, we didn't speak. Just as we were approaching the airport, he asked me where I was going. I told him I was going to Whitehorse in the Yukon Territory. He asked, "Why in hell would you go to the Yukon?" I told him I was going to play hockey up there. He joked that he hoped that I had put on long underwear this morning. He actually turned out to be a really nice guy, and for the 15 or so minutes that we had left in the trip, we had a good conversation.

CHAPTER 22

New Horizons

I had a two-hour flight to Vancouver, then a two-hour layover until the flight to Whitehorse. Two hours later, for the second time in my life, I was on a flight to Whitehorse, but this time I was staying put. When I arrived in Whitehorse, it was -10°C and snowing. When I left California, it was 104°F. Talk about culture shock. Art picked me up at the airport, and our first stop was to see Bloski. I hadn't seen him for awhile so it would be good to catch up. He had operated a sandwich shop on the main drive, and that's where we went to meet up with him. We went into the shop. Mike was behind the counter with a towel over his shoulder. I remembered the first time I saw him, with his ill-fitting shirt and tie and his cigar. We got caught up, and he told me what to expect playing there. Nothing out of the ordinary. We said our goodbyes and that was the last time I ever saw him. I hope he's doing well. He's quite a character and a really good guy.

Next, Art took me to Beaver Lumber, where I would be working. I spoke with Chuck Corothers, who was the assistant manager. Don and Karen Corothers, Chuck's father and Stepmother were the owners of the store. Chuck told me it was the #1 Beaver Lumber store for sales in Canada. I thought that was most impressive. He said I could start in the yard on Monday, so that would give me the weekend to get settled. He also said he had a hockey team for me to play for. Whitehorse had their own senior league, and Beaver Lumber sponsored a team. Their goalie was injured at the moment, and he was hoping that I could sub in. I told him I would be happy to. Our next stop was to where I would be staying. Rob Krauzig was a member of the executive, and he had a room to rent. The room had a bed and a dresser, and since I had been living out of my suitcase, it was all I needed. Rob was about my age and worked in a warehouse. He didn't have many rules other than, "keep the place clean." Turns out he was quite anal about it. It was not an easy rule for me to follow. I had always been a slob when it came to keeping house. We would be quite the "Oscar and Felix" duo. I know it drove Rob around the bend sometimes, but I did my best.

It was mid-October, and the season hadn't started yet. Practices were Monday and Wednesday. When I arrived in Whitehorse, Art and I waited at the baggage carousel for my hockey equipment. When I had left San Francisco, my hockey bag was intact. It was a huge bag, made of cloth and was big enough to hold all my equipment, pads included. One of the baggage handlers at one of the airports must have been The Incredible Hulk because when Art and I saw the bag come around, the straps were missing. They had been attached to the bag with these large rivets. The rivets were there, but no straps. I could see one coming off if you tried to lift the whole bag by that one strap. But to rip both of them off, you had to be either super strong or really stupid, or you hated hockey players and ripped them off on purpose. When I arrived at practice for the first time, the players who were there had a good laugh when I walked in dragging my bag by one end.

I found an empty spot on the bench and one by one the players all came up to me and introduced themselves. Jay

Trout, Blair Brieman, Jordan Borgford, (I would call him "Jordy Borgy"), Jay Glass, Steve Nelson, Shelby Workman, Steve Smith, Derek and Ian Kuster, Ray Quock, Doug Cook, Darryl Sturko and a few others. I then met Dennis Salamandyk, the other goalie. He had an easy-going manner with that underlying confidence. He was very friendly and had a quick smile. Dennis had a story similar to mine but much more impressive. He was from Thompson, Manitoba. He had started playing organized hockey at the age of 16. Two years later, he was playing for the Medicine Hat Tigers in the Western League, and my good friend Kelly Hrudey was his goaltending partner. In his second season, he had been traded to Spokane and instead of going there, he decided to go home but received a job offer in Whitehorse and had been there ever since. We had played against him three years prior when we came up with the Rebels. He hadn't made much of an impression on me then, but that would change. Denny's birth date turned out to be 4 days after mine. He always made a big deal about me being 4 days older than him so he called me "Grandpa." I, in return, called him "Junior."

Early that first season in Whitehorse a defenseman joined our team. His name was Derek MacPherson. He was very engaging. He always seemed to have something interesting to say. I could talk to him seemingly forever about any subject. He was just a really smart, interesting guy. After about a month of knowing him, we were on a flight to Fairbanks and he told me about his brother Duncan. Duncan MacPherson was an outstanding junior player with the Saskatoon Blades and became a first-round draft pick of the New York Islanders. After a few seasons in the minors The Islanders bought out his contract and Duncan accepted a player/coach offer from a professional team is Scotland. On his way there he stopped to do some snowboarding in Austria. He never came down off the mountain. After he didn't show up in Scotland at the arranged time, his parents reported him missing. The story I was told was that the man who ran the rental shop stated that Duncan had returned his snowboard and that was the last time anyone saw him. His disappearance was a complete mystery and there were many rumours about what had happened to him. At the time Derek told me this story, his brother had been missing for about 2 years. You could tell it really ate at him not knowing what happened to Duncan. I couldn't imagine what I would do if one of my family members just disappeared without a trace. I have to give Derek all the credit in the world for being able to keep it together. A lesser man would've folded like a tent. In 2003 a resort employee saw a glove sticking out of the snow on one of the runs. It turned out to be Duncan. His snowboard was found with his body. The investigation into his disappearance was a boondoggle from the start and was even worse after his body was found. I haven't spoken to Derek about this, he left our team sometime during my first season in Whitehorse, but I wish nothing but the best for him and his family.

I was hoping that the change of scenery would help me bump my slump. And it did. Sort of. I still didn't have my game back, but it was getting there. In my first practice with the team, as usual, I watched the other goalie. Denny was pretty intense during practice. He didn't want anyone to score on him, and he worked really hard. He had almost an obsession with stopping the puck. It made me realize how lazy my own practice habits had been, and I figured I was going to have to pull up my bootstraps just to keep pace. I found it difficult. As hard as I tried, practice just wasn't the same as a game, and I needed that competition. I couldn't just make it up in my head. I finally decided that Denny and I were just different, no better or worse, just different. I would continue to march to my drummer, and he to his.

I settled pretty easily into life in Whitehorse. I was a city boy back in the city. At least, it felt that way. It was more of a large town than a small city, with a population of 23,000 people. I started my job at Beaver Lumber and enjoyed it. I made a good wage, and the job was interesting. I could probably write another book about the people who worked there. They were all characters. It was cold in Whitehorse, like Saskatchewan. They say that Whitehorse has 4 seasons, but 3 of them are winter. One difference between Assiniboia and Whitehorse was that Whitehorse had a McDonalds, and any other store you could ask for. The downside was, it was expensive to live there. If you wanted to buy a new car for instance, it was cheaper to fly to Edmonton and drive the car back, than it was to buy the same car in Whitehorse. But it was a pleasant place to live, and it was beautiful. In the winter, when the sun was going down, the city would be dark, but the mountain across the Yukon River would still be in sunlight. It looked like the mountain was glowing from the inside. Also, a few times a year, you would see the Aurora Borealis. One really cold night, it covered the whole sky, and I swear you could hear it crackling.

Rob Borud was the GM of the Huskies and the driving force behind getting the team off the ground, and also for putting the league together. He was a successful businessman in Whitehorse and had a love for the game. I'm not sure if he ever played, but you could tell he was a big fan. He had hired Art in the summer. It was a strong front office, and I was excited to see who else they would bring in. Scott Binner was still trying out for a team in Dayton, Ohio in the East Coast Hockey League, and Art said he wasn't really happy with his situation and that he was trying to get him to come up. That would be awesome. Jay Glass, who had played at UBC, had speed to burn. Binner was a little faster than him in straight ahead speed, but Jay was quicker in his lateral moves and had more of a scoring touch. It would be fun to see both of them drive teams crazy.

Whitehorse had two radio stations, and they were going to share the broadcasting rights to the Huskies games. The A.M. station was going to broadcast the Friday games and the F.M. station the Saturday games. The A.M. station had a one-hour sports talk show every Thursday night at 7 o'clock. Shortly after I arrived in town, Evan Burr, the sports director, invited me to be on the show. I told him to get lost. I'm kidding. I couldn't wait and was excited to do my first radio interview. When I got there, he got me set up in the room opposite his. We could see each other through the glass. I had headphones and a microphone and a bottle of water. He went through all the sporting headlines for the day and then got to me. We talked about my history and how I had started when I was 18, and about my time in Assiniboia and Fresno. Twice during the hour, they gave away prizes if you could answer a trivia question. The first one came 20 minutes into the interview. The caller answered the trivia question correctly and won the prize. Evan then asked the caller, "Do you have any questions for Jerry Hack, goaltender of the Whitehorse Huskies?" After a brief pause, the caller simply said, "No." Evan and I laughed and continued the interview. 20 minutes later, it was time to give another prize away. Evan asked the trivia question and a call poured in. Again, the caller answered the question correctly and won the prize. Once again, Evan asked the caller, "Do you have any questions for Jerry Hack?" This time there was an even briefer pause, and the caller said, "No." I said, "It's moments like these that keep you humble."

One of Rob and Art's first acquisitions was Darren Livingston, a defenseman from Manitoba who joined the team shortly after the season began. His claim to fame was that he held the career penalty minute record for this Junior B league he played in back home. The first time I laid eyes on the guy, I felt sorry for him. I thought he was ugly. He was under 6 feet tall, about 190 pounds, and he had long brown hair that was like wire, and he looked like he hadn't showered, ever. My first thought was, "This guy will never get laid." He had a mouth like a sewer. Everything he said was laced with profanity. Hockey players are known for being uncouth, but this guy took it to a new level. Now, contrary to my belief that he wouldn't be a hit with the ladies, nothing could be further from the truth. The women just flocked to the guy. Women who I'd give my eye teeth to go out with, were fawning all over him. Talk about animal magnetism. I was at a party one night and this attractive girl who was going gaga over him was standing next to me. I asked her what the attraction was, she looked at me and gave that quick little raise of the eyebrows and said, "mmmmm… bad boy." This was true, he was a bad boy. He had over 1,400 minutes, (or so he says), in penalties in that junior league in Manitoba. I can't say I doubted him. When you spoke to Darren you liked him, but you could tell he was a little left of center. The dots didn't quite connect for the guy. We were partying in a hotel room once, and he got it into his head that he was going to hang from the ceiling fan and spin around. He thought it would be funny, and we would all laugh our asses off. He jumped up and grabbed onto the spinning blades, and of course they broke. He fell to the floor on his back, and we all thought it was funny, and we laughed our asses off. I don't know how he thought that hanging from the ceiling fan was even possible. He wanted to go Dog Sledding, but instead of using regular sled dogs he wanted to use dachshunds, or as he called them, "dink dogs." He may not have been splitting the atom in his spare time, but he was not a bad hockey player. He did have some ability and could play at the senior level. During this one game, we were playing in Fairbanks. I don't remember what the score was, but we were probably winning because Denny was playing in net for us. I was on the bench, working the gate closest to center ice. Darren was playing left defense, and the play was in the Gold Kings zone. The puck came to him at the point, which put him directly in front of the Gold Kings bench. He wound up for a slapshot, and as he did, somebody from the Gold Kings said something he didn't like, because he let go of his stick during his backswing, which caused the stick to go about 20 feet in the air, and if you can imagine a WWE wrestler diving off the top rope, that is what Darren did. He took two strides and dove, spread eagle, into the Gold Kings bench. What I remember seeing is his stick 20 feet in the air, and then looking at the Gold Kings bench, which I could see clearly through the glass, and seeing Darren swinging with both fists. He had knocked one player backwards onto the floor behind the bench and about 5 others were all over him, but they couldn't pin his arms, and he was just flailing away. One guy tried to grab him from behind but Darren elbowed him in the mouth and chipped the guy's tooth. All of our players who were on the ice at the time, were now trying to get into the Gold Kings bench, and the melee just became a mass of humanity. The linesmen AND the referee climbed into the bench to pull everyone off of him. It took them probably five minutes to extricate Darren from the Gold Kings bench. In the meantime, the Gold King players are all taking potshots at him. Finally, the linesmen got him out of there and were escorting him back to our bench, so he could go to the dressing room. He had this shit-eating grin on his face, and I swear to God this is true, he didn't have a mark on him. He came out of that melee completely unscathed, while at least three of their guys had to go to the dressing room to get bandaged up. The fans were apoplectic. All of them were yelling profanities at him and calling him every name in the book. I tried to open the gate for him, but I was laughing so hard it took me a couple of tries. As he was standing there he winked and said, "That was fuckin' fun eh?" I couldn't say a word, I couldn't breathe. After the game, he was the talk of the town. We went to the bar and the women just flocked to the guy. Darren Livingston. Bad boy.

Tom Dobos was from Hungary, and he had been a star player for the Hungarian national team, which caught the eye of some NHL scouts. Tom had been sent to the East Coast Hockey League's Nashville Knights. They sent him to us to teach him "North American" hockey. Apparently, Tom didn't like the body checking part of the game, and they asked the Huskies to "toughen him up." Tom barely spoke English at the beginning, but he was a pretty smart guy and picked it up fairly quickly. He particularly liked the phrase, "Fuck you asshole," from the movie, *The Terminator*. Tom quickly showed why he had been scouted. Neither Denny or I could stop him in practice. He scored at will and made it look easy. Most hockey players you can read like a book, especially when you practice against them so often. But not Tommy. He was a complete and utter mystery every time he shot the puck. Denny and I would put our heads together and try to come up with some strategy that we could use against the guy, but absolutely nothing worked. We eventually just gave up trying. We gave Tommy the nickname, "2 Guns," because it seemed like he was shooting 2 pucks at once, and we always tried to stop the wrong one. As the season got going, the reason he was sent to us became abundantly clear. He was petrified of getting hit. He had such a tight grip on his stick it should've turned to sawdust in his hands. By the end of the season, he had scored a total of 2 goals. We changed his nickname to Tommy "2 goals" Dobos. He is, to this day, the greatest practice player I have ever seen.

The season had started, and we played a few league games against Fairbanks and Anchorage. Anchorage was led by Keith Street, who had been a star with the University of Alaska at Anchorage and goalie Chad Mehoff. The Fairbanks fans, I was told, had a great time with Chad Mehoff's name. During my tenure with the Huskies, I think we only beat Fairbanks one time, at home, and we beat the Aces, at home, once. They both were really strong teams, and Anchorage was probably a little bit better than Fairbanks at this time. We also played teams from Seattle, and Penticton.

I don't really remember how the games went early that first season in Whitehorse. I remember that I was hot and cold. Good game, bad game. But Art had promised me half the starts, and his word was his bond. He knew I would pull out of it eventually. It's doubly difficult to shake a slump when you are on a new team, and nobody knows who you are. In contrast, Denny was lights out. The guy was incredible. He could scramble like no one I had ever seen. He could contort his body like Gumby and made miraculous saves time and again. He won a few games for us basically on his own. I was just hoping to not lose any on my own.

Binner arrived in November, and we got reacquainted. It was good to have a friend on the team. I was getting to know the other guys, but I hadn't earned their respect yet. I was working hard in practice and was starting to feel better. Hopefully, I would get it together before the Russians arrived.

More players arrived in November, and there were less and less local guys on the team. There was defensemen Ken

Watson, whose older brothers Joe and Jim played with the Philadelphia Flyers during the Broad Street Bullies era. Shawn Lofroth, and Todd Granley, as well as the addition of Ron Servatius, who could play both forward and defense, the local guys could see the writing on the wall. Jay Trout decided to leave the team, while Derek Kuster and Steve Smith stayed around, even though they knew they might not play much. It made for an interesting mix but also became a point of contention. The fans might not support the team if there were not many local guys on it. Rob and Art had to walk a fine line between getting good players and keeping enough local talent to satisfy the paying customers. Some of the local guys were long on heart but short on skill. But whatever they had to give; they gave. You could never fault their effort. They were all heart and soul guys. It was never going to be the brotherhood like we had in Assiniboia, but we did have our moments.

Brieman and Glass hated each other, and this caused a divide in the dressing room. Some guys were friends with Glass, and some were friends with Brieman. It came to a head in the airport on one of our road trips. The two almost came to blows. Servatius managed to step in between them and get them to settle down. The hard feelings would last the rest of my time in Whitehorse.

Finally, December came, and the Russians were in town. They had played 3 games in Anchorage, 3 games in Fairbanks, and were now in Whitehorse for 3 more before heading home. They had won every game, except for one tie against Anchorage. It was a huge event. Takhini Arena was sold out for all 3 games. Fifteen hundred people would be in the stands. All 3 games would be videotaped for a documentary about the Huskies that was being filmed.

One thing that was different about the Huskies, and something that no other Senior Team had, was a female trainer. Her name was Lynn, and at the risk of sounding sexist, she was beautiful which was not just my opinion. She would often accompany the team on road trips and whenever we went out, she would turn heads everywhere. Nobody had the guts to approach her because she was with 25 guys, but you could see guys look, ogle and whisper to each other and point. The medical stuff she knew backwards and forwards, and she took really good care of us. All the guys treated her like a sister and were very protective of her. There was a respect factor, and no player on our team would ever even come close to crossing the line with her. Even Darren Livingston, who never in his life learned the meaning of the word "restraint" would dial it back while she was around. And Lynn was tough. During games, Lynn and I would often stand beside each other, behind the bench, in the entryway to the hall that led to the dressing rooms. One game, a puck was shot into our bench, missed me by inches and hit Lynn right in the face, and she dropped like a stone. I thought she was dead. She had to go to the hospital for treatment, but luckily it was just a badly bruised orbital bone and she was back the next night with this huge black eye. Before the Russia series began, she was introduced to the Russian delegation as our "trainer." The Russians all raised their eyebrows and looked at each other in shock. Apparently, in Russian, trainer means coach. We had to explain to them that she was the medical trainer and didn't actually coach the team.

The first game against the Russians took place, on Dec 2, 1991. The stands were jammed, and they had some pregame ceremonies. Notably, the player introductions. Trevor Haggard, the P.A. announcer, had a lot of trouble with the Russian names, but he managed to slog through.

Nobody could tell you if he butchered the names or said them perfectly. When it became our turn, they had us skate out from where the ice cleaner entered and exited the rink. They had spotlights and dry ice and they played the "Theme from Rocky" as we were introduced. Very cheesy. The players all hated it. We were all introduced and skated to the blue line to line up for the National Anthems. The Soviet Union was in the midst of breaking up while these games were going on, and the Russians really did not look happy while their anthem was being played. But then again, they didn't look happy most of the time. The ceremonial drop of the puck and then away we went. Denny played the first game, I was to play the second, and we were to split the third. The first period started and you could tell that everyone was nervous. Except Denny. He was in his element. He made saves early and often, while we were mostly standing around in awe. The Russians, we were told, were the 2nd Division Central Red Army team, and a few of them had even played with the big team. They were all soldiers in the army, but they were a professional hockey team. They made plays that were not typical of senior teams, and they seemed to always have the puck. I think the score after the first period was 2-0 Russia. During the first intermission, right after the ice clean, they brought out this massive carpet and put it on the ice. Then out came the Yukon dancers. There were about a dozen of them who were dressed in 1850's costumes. They did a 5 to 10-minute performance and then left the ice. When they tried to pull the carpet up, the foam backing had frozen to the ice. When they finally got it up, most of the foam backing stayed down. They tried to scrape it off and even brought the ice cleaning machine out again, but to no avail. That stuff just wasn't going to leave easily. There was this huge rectangular patch on the ice in front of the penalty boxes that was off colour. Every time the puck went into this area, it slowed down. When players skated through it, they would have to clean off their skate blades after the shift was over. It was most definitely amateur night in the Yukon.

When the second period began, it was much the same as the first. Denny was at his best, but it wasn't enough. They were just too strong. The weirdest thing was, when they scored a goal, they didn't celebrate. They just kind of congregated for a couple of seconds, and then went to center ice. There was never a reaction from their bench. The Russian players were like robots. It was like they weren't allowed to celebrate or the KGB (as far as I could tell there were two KGB agents. They were humourless guys who often kept to themselves) would arrest them. In contrast, when we scored, it was like Mardi Gras. I think the score after the second period was 5-1.

The third period was a little bit better for us. We had stopped standing around and actually began playing. We had more puck possession and also showed them a little bit of "North American" hockey. We started hitting them. That seemed to slow them down a little bit. They didn't like it. We scored a couple of goals, but so did they. We ended up losing 7-3. But we felt like our best was yet to come.

The second game was played the next night. Dec. 3rd, 1991. A week before my 30th birthday. I was nervous but not overly so. I always enjoyed playing in front of big crowds. We did the same pregame ceremonies as the first game. When the game started, our players were standing around watching again. I made some good saves and was feeling confident. I remembered Grant Fuhr saying that the Russians really like to hang on to the puck and make you move first. This was proven to me when they got a breakaway. I tried to be as patient as possible. The guy made a move, and I just went with him and when he got in too deep, he never even took a shot. He just kept the puck and peeled away and kept the play going. About ten minutes into the game, they struck first. A guy came in from my left, faked a shot, then shot right away and snuck it through my legs as I was moving. A few minutes later, they got another chance. This time the guy dragged the puck across the front of the net and tucked it underneath me. I ended up on my stomach and saw the puck cross the line and settle in the back of the net. The puck was within reach, and I just reacted. I grabbed the puck from the back of the net and pulled it underneath my chest. Brieman was yelling at the ref, "No goal, no goal!" The ref came skating over and said, "Did I say it was a goal?" When I stood up, the puck was underneath me of course. The referee indicated face off in our end. Brieman and I shared a laugh. I definitely got away with that one. I think the only person in the rink who didn't see it go in was the referee. The fans down at that end of the rink even booed me just a little. The Russians never said a word, they just lined up for the faceoff. They would score another before the end of the period. We would enter the second period down 2-0, just like the previous night. Unlike the previous night, we started playing our game to start the second period, and Jay Glass scored a beautiful goal on a breakaway. Jay got so excited, he jumped into Blair Brieman's arms and the two fell to the ice. They hated each other, but they were so happy to score, I guess it didn't matter in that moment, and all that other shit could wait. With the score 2-1 and us playing better, the game became intense. It stayed 2-1 for the rest of the period. I made some really good saves and finally felt like my old self again. Hopefully, this would be the end of my slump. The third period started, and we scored the tying goal. At least we thought so. As it turned out, we had hit the post and then the net came off its moorings. The puck never did cross the goal line. A little while later, they scored to make it 3-1. With about 8 minutes to go, Doug Cook delivered the best hip check I have ever seen. The guy received a pass from his right, and just turned to head up ice when Cook bent over and the guy went ass over teakettle and slammed down to the ice. After the game, we watched it over and over on the video. It was perfectly executed and legal. The guy got up, went straight to the dressing room, and we never saw him again. I could hear Bob Cole in my head saying, "They're going home!" Shortly after that hit, we scored to make it 3-2. And we were gaining momentum. The Russians only carried one goalie, and we thought that he must be getting tired after almost 8 straight games. But try as we might we couldn't tie the game. They scored another one late, and the game ended 4-2 Russians. We still felt like we had more to give, and the next night would hopefully end up in our favour.

In between the second and third game, the Russians were at the mall, selling Russian made souvenirs to the locals. They had a big long table full of these little trinkets and nesting dolls. One of the customs officers from the airport was at the mall on their day off. This person saw the items on display and that they were selling them. This person immediately rushed home to get their uniform on and went back to the mall and shut them down. Apparently, there was some duty, or tax, or levy, or tariff, that wasn't paid, and Canada could not survive without the $4,000 that needed to be collected. Like I said before, the Soviet Union was crumbling at this very moment, and times were extremely tough in the motherland. All the Russian players wore old hockey equipment that was barely adequate. Some of them used packing tape on their sticks. Their jerseys were bottom of the barrel, old type Montreal Canadiens jerseys without the logo. They were just trying to drum up some cash to help offset some of the expenses that they were incurring. But some low-level bureaucrat saw a rule being broken and needed to act. It was a disgusting display of government interference, and the whole Husky organization from top to bottom was extremely embarrassed, to say the least. We took up a collection to make up for the transgression and made a formal apology to the Russian delegation. The Russians did not want to accept the money. They're reasoning was that when they were in Alaska, they sold their goods at the malls, and there was no problem. But they should have known that when they entered Canada, the rules might be different, and that they should have contacted the authorities to find out what those rules might have been. It was their responsibility and that they would accept the consequences. We said bullshit to that. We insisted that this customs officer had overstepped their bounds, and that this is definitely not the way Canadians treat their guests. We insisted that they take the money, and they reluctantly agreed. I hope that the customs officer involved in this story reads this book. The people of Whitehorse all know who you are, and hope you feel shame. Peckerhead.

The third game started the next night, December 4th, 1991. Denny would start this game, and I would come in halfway through and finish. We did the same pregame ritual, which the players hated, and then finally, time for the opening faceoff. Our team got off to a good start for once. We actually got the lead, and the game went back and forth for the first period. The game was tied by the end of it. Everybody was playing well, but Denny was playing out of his mind. During the second period, when the time was approaching for me to enter the game, I considered telling Art just to let Denny continue playing, and I should have. But I had invited a lot of friends to watch the game and told them that I'd be coming in halfway through. To my regret, I entered the game with about nine and a half minutes left to go in the second period. We were ahead 4-3 at that point. By the time there was 6 minutes left in the period, we were down 6-4. They scored on three of their first four shots I faced. I made a couple of saves after that, and as the play continued, the puck was in our zone, when a pass was made to the defenseman at the point to my left. He one-timed a shot, and as I was drifting over, I reacted by sliding over on my knees. The shot hit me on the underneath part of my jock. I saw a white flash of light, and I had never felt such pain. I don't remember much after that, but my friends said that I just leaned forward slowly until my forehead hit the ice. I was in the fetal position, but on my knees and elbows with my forehead still on the ice, and my hands covering the back of my head. I couldn't breathe. Every man in the building went ooohhhh!! The whistle blew and our trainer, Lynn, came out to see me along with Denny. My stomach felt like it was going to explode, and I couldn't catch my breath. The trainer and Denny were asking me questions, but I couldn't answer. Finally, I was able to catch a little breath and told them that I just needed a minute. 1 minute turned into about 5, but I was able to finally get up and return to play. I really don't remember the game after that. My friends told me that I made this mind-blowing save that nobody could believe, but I don't remember and I couldn't tell you if it was true or not without watching the video. And to this day, I have never watched the Game 3 video. It's way too painful to even think about. About halfway through the third, we were down 7 to 4, and I couldn't continue. I was cramping up so bad that I couldn't move. There was about 12 minutes left in the third period, and Denny came back into the game. When I got to the dressing room and took my jock off, it was shattered into a hundred pieces. It was only held together by the thin foam padding on the outside.

I keep it as a reminder of what can happen if you lose focus. Again, Denny was incredible, and nobody scored after I left, and Denny was rightfully awarded the player of the game. Final score 7-4 Russia. I have very few regrets in my life, but not letting Denny finish that game is one of the biggest ones I have. It bothers me even now. I should've listened to my inner voice. I have no doubt that we would've won if I had stayed on the bench. I would never make that mistake again, and from that point on, I have always listened to that inner voice. But I must say, the overall experience of playing against the Russians was once in a lifetime and one that I will never forget.

After the Russian series, my 30th birthday and Christmas came and went, also New Year's. In January, we had a road trip to Assiniboia, back to my old stomping grounds. I was very excited. It would be good to see Terrie, and everyone again. Binner had returned to Saskatchewan after the Russia series. He didn't like the team dynamic and wanted to return home. I couldn't blame him. It was a tough adjustment living in the north. Denny had work commitments and couldn't make the trip, so we brought one of the Midget goalies just as a backup. I was going to play both games. It was so weird walking into the visitors dressing room. It was so small, I had trouble getting dressed. It was just too cramped. The first game was Friday night. A good crowd came to see Art and I challenge our old team. The game was a tight checking affair, and we came out on top 2-1. I had one of my better games. Frank Hamel came up to me and said, "What the fuck do you think you're doing, playing that well?" That made me happy.

That night we partied in the Bar-B. I guess they had taken back sponsorship of the team. I had a great time getting reacquainted with everyone, and I got to see Terrie for the first time in months. The next night we got creamed, 10-1. My up and down season continued.

Later that January, Whitehorse hosted the 1992 Arctic Winter Games. Athletes from all over northern Canada participated. Whitehorse entered a hockey team. I wasn't considered a resident since I had only been there a few months, so I was ineligible. Denny didn't play either, I don't remember why. I went to watch all of the hockey games that Whitehorse played. I was watching this one game from the corner of the rink. I was by myself with no one around me. This young boy, maybe 9 or 10 came up to me and asked, "Are you Jerry Hack?" I told him I was. He started rapid firing questions at me about where I was from, who I had played for, who I had played against, who was my favourite player, etc. etc. It was like MaCaulay Culkin in "Uncle Buck." I felt like asking him what was his record was for consecutive questions. He finally got to the end of the inquisition and then he looked up at me with total awe and said, "You're the second-best goalie in the Yukon!" I just laughed, and said, "Yeah, Denny's pretty good, isn't he?" And the boy nodded his head and answered, "Mmm…hmmmm" in the affirmative. In my head, I was thinking, "Thanks a lot kid, no autograph for you."

In February we had a road trip into Alberta to play the Stony Plain Eagles, and when we were on our way back, we had the usual layover in Vancouver. Rob Borud had booked a trip to Mexico. While the team was in the airport, Rob and I, and a couple of other players were walking along and chatting, and then he had to go to a different boarding gate, and we went to ours. That was the last time any of us ever saw him. While swimming in the ocean in Mexico, he got caught in an undercurrent and drowned. The lifeguards brought him back on the beach and tried to resuscitate him, but to no avail. I know at least one of his brothers was there. R.I.P Rogie, and thank you for everything you did for us. We played with black armbands on our jerseys the rest of the year. In March, the documentary about our team came out. It was shown across Canada on the CBC Newsworld channel. Aside from those of us that were associated with the team, I only met one other person who ever saw it. The documentary was called, *'Breaking Trail with the Whitehorse Huskies.'* It was dedicated to Rob Borud, and was pretty well done, I thought.

On our last road trip for the season, we flew to Fairbanks one more time. We boarded the good old DC-3. As usual on that plane, the passengers board first, and the pilots board after everyone is settled in and ready to go. The night before, Blair Brieman, and a few of the others watched the movie *Alive!* about the soccer team in South America whose plane had crashed in the Andes Mountains. They resorted to cannibalism to survive. When the pilots finally boarded our plane, (they both looked to be about 25 or so), Brieman said to them, "If you crash, we're eating you first." Both the pilots looked at Brieman like he had a penis growing out of his forehead.

Hockey players are not known for their intelligence, but some can actually be downright obtuse. After playing in Fairbanks on the Friday night, some of us were sitting in the hotel restaurant Saturday afternoon when one of the guys came running up to the table we were at and stated emphatically, "They're talking about us on ESPN!!" Someone said "no way." I won't name the individual who was bringing us this exciting news flash, but his initials are T.G. and they said, "Absolutely, they're talking about the Yukon Huskies, and it was at least a few minutes long." One of the guys sitting at the table had to explain to T.G. that the Yukon Huskies ESPN was talking about were actually the University of Connecticut Huskies, also known as the UConn Huskies. T.G. wasn't even embarrassed. He thought it was cool.

My first season in Whitehorse ended on an up note. In our last game of the season, we defeated the Anchorage Aces at home. I don't remember the score, but I played really well and so did the team in front of me. We didn't have a season ending awards banquet, but Denny was hands down our MVP. I thought he should have been playing pro somewhere. If not down in the States, then over in Europe. He was just too good. With all due respect to Komo and Bloski, Denny was absolutely the best goalie I ever played with or against.

In April, I received an invitation to play in the Native Tournament. Ray Quock had asked me to join his team, The Nannock Warriors. It sounded like a lot of fun. Each team was allowed two non-native players. I don't think the Warriors asked a second guy. I had a blast. The guys on the team were awesome. They treated me like I had been on the team forever. We went all the way to the final but lost to Denny's team from Lower Post, I think it was called. The atmosphere was wild, 1,500 first nations people, banging their drums and chanting. It was like something out of a movie. I was hoping to play for the Warriors again the next year.

CHAPTER 23

The Good, The Bad, and The End

The summer of 1992, I stayed in Whitehorse. My job had been going well, and I wanted to see the midnight sun. It was cool, but it really messes with you. You think it's about 9:00 at night, but it's really 11:00 and you need to get to bed. In the middle of summer, at "night", it kind of gets to dusk for about an hour and a half, and then it's a bright sunny day again. Weekends were awesome, but if you had to work the next day, it kind of sucked.

I played slow pitch baseball that summer for the first time ever. Weird thing about me, I can hit a golf ball 300 yards, (not every time, but I can do it), but I can't hit a baseball. I can barely get it to the outfield. But I had fun and met a lot of fun people. This one girl, her name was Joanne, but everyone called her Josie, had a great sense of humour and could keep us in stitches for hours. I also borrowed my roommate Rob's mountain bike pretty much every day. He had a bad back that whole summer so he wasn't using it anyway. I wasn't going to sit on my ass and take it easy. I was going to work my ass off and get into the best shape of my life. I was going to prove to everybody that the previous season was just a "one off," and show them what I was really made of. There was no summer hockey, so I did the next best thing and rode a bike all summer. Terrie had finally moved to Whitehorse so I moved out of Rob's place, and we got an apartment together. I got her a job at Beaver Lumber, and all was good.

In September, the ice went back in at the rinks around town. The team had some informal scrimmages. And I felt great. I finally felt like I was back to my old self again. Denny was busy with work, so he didn't partake in any of these scrimmages at first. In early October, when things started to get going, we were scheduled for a three-day training camp. I couldn't wait, but beforehand, I got some bad news. Art Birss would not be coaching, I didn't know why, and I never really got a good answer. Art was always in my corner. He was the only coach who really believed in me. Everyone else would look at my resume and just assume I wasn't any good. It didn't seem to matter how I played, they just saw that I never played junior hockey and that was that. Even Rob Borud had a little bit of "Volsky-itis," he was just enamored with Mike Bloski and always compared my resume to Mike's.

Greg Anderson, who was our captain the previous year, would retain that title, but also be a playing coach. Ron Areshnikoff would be the head coach. I could almost feel the knife blade drawing out. "Time to make some cuts!" Is what was going through my head. Well, I figured there was nothing I could do about it but play well enough so that they couldn't cut me. There were about 5 goalies in camp, but none of them could touch Denny or me. I was safe for the time being.

The really big news was that Whitehorse was going to host the Allan Cup. The Senior AAA Canadian Championship was going to be held in our town. This was extremely exciting. For senior hockey players, it's the pinnacle. It's our own version of the Stanley Cup. I knew we were going to have to bring in some players, and most likely another top flight goalie, but hey, I didn't mind being the third goalie on an Allan Cup winning team. I was pumped, and so was Denny.

We had some games in October, and Denny was lights out as usual. I didn't get as many starts, but I got a good share, especially on the road. It was in Ron and Greg's best interests to keep me happy, because Denny's work schedule was getting busier and he wasn't going to be able to make some of the road trips. And there was no other goalie in town who could play at this level and had enough free time to commit to the team.

We went to Fairbanks on our first road trip of the season. Assiniboia, Stony Plain, and Abbotsford had all dropped out of the league, so it was just us, Fairbanks and Anchorage for this season. These two games against Fairbanks would lead to the proudest moment of my hockey career. Denny couldn't make the trip, so again we brought along a Midget goalie for insurance. I would again play both games. I had new pads this season. Wayne Cousins, who was a young successful businessman in town and president of the Huskies, got them for me off of "the internet." I had never heard of this "internet" thing before, but apparently you could get anything you wanted. He ordered these pads for me, and they were the best pads I had ever had up to that point. They were foam filled and light as a feather. Rebound control was a bit of a problem, but something I could figure out. When the Friday night game started, a Gold Kings player came across the blueline and let go a slapshot. I went down in the butterfly and kicked the shot out. The sound of the puck hitting my pad made a small "booommm" that echoed. All 2,000 people went, "oooooooohhhhh." It was funny, and I had to laugh a bit. The whole first period seemed to be played in our end of the rink. It was like a shooting gallery, but as Woody Harrelson said in "White Men Can't Jump," I was "in the zone." And every time we got the puck down in their end we scored. We were up 3-0 after the first period. The second period was much like the first. They were all over us, and they just kept firing the puck at me. I was able to hold them off for a while, but eventually they managed to get a couple by me. The score at the end of the second was 4-2 for us. The third period was more of the same, shot after shot. Save after save. I felt so good. The Gold King players were getting frustrated. They started slamming their sticks on the ice and looking up to the rafters. But the great ending wasn't to be. They kept pouring it on and eventually tied the score. They scored the winning goal in overtime. I just couldn't keep my finger in the dyke any longer. The shots were 58 to 15, and we lost 5-4. I didn't have to hear the "Hey Goalie" chant until the very end.

The next night we are on the ice for warm ups. I am on the ice at the end of our bench right at the blue line doing my stretches, when I hear from behind me, "Hey Jerry!" I look up, and one of their fans had climbed the glass and was half the way over. He reached down his hand and said, "I just wanted to shake your hand, that was a great game last night! So much fun to watch!" I took my glove off and shook his hand. I barely got out a "thank you," before he jumped down and was gone. The game went similarly to the night before, only this time, I wasn't quite as sharp at the beginning. We fell behind 3-0 in the first period. The second period was still more shots, but I had settled in and they weren't getting any by me. I was back in the zone. We managed to claw back to 3-2 by the end of the second. The third period, we tied it up. The game was still being played mostly in our end, but we would get the odd scoring chance. But the script went like the previous night. Fairbanks scored with just over 5 minutes remaining to go up 4-3 and then added an empty net goal with less than a minute to go. Final score 5-3. Shots were 55 to 20. I had stopped 104 out of 112 shots. I stopped 92.8

percent of the shots they took in the two games. Which in senior hockey, is about as good as it gets. I've told you how raucous the Fairbanks fans are. They will say almost anything to get you off your game, and they are relentless and ruthless. After the game was over, the P.A. announcer said over the speakers, "Ladies and gentlemen, Jerry Hack stopped 104 out of 112 shots this weekend. How about giving him a round of applause?" To my astonishment, all 2,000 fans stood up and applauded for about a minute. I could barely believe it. It was, and is, the proudest moment of my hockey career. Some of their players and coaches, and even their trainer, came over to shake my hand. John Rosie, who was president of their team came into our dressing room to congratulate me. We chatted for about 10 minutes. The next time we went to Fairbanks, the fans were back to booing me, and insulting my family. Situation normal, and I wouldn't have it any other way.

The disappointing thing about the weekend was first, that we lost both games, and second, in Monday's newspaper, the reporter for the Whitehorse newspaper (who I was on very good terms with) wrote about the games, but didn't even mention my name. I doubt that anybody who had read it would have known that I was even there. I called the reporter and asked him why he hadn't mentioned me. I didn't do it because I liked seeing my name in the paper, but because I felt that my spot on the team was in danger. I needed all the help I could get and a little bit of positive ink could go a long way. I felt Ron and Greg, who had both played junior and pro, were not in my corner and were actively looking for someone else. The reporter kind of just stumbled and bumbled and hummed and hawed but didn't really have a valid reason for omitting my performance. I asked him not to write anything about me calling him and complaining. I didn't want it getting back to the coaches. He agreed.

The next weekend we had home games. Denny started the Friday night game and was average, (by his standards), and he also started the next night, and was average again. I was a little shaken that I didn't start the second game after my performance the previous weekend, and I went to see Greg on Monday where he worked. I asked him what was up. And he said that I played well the previous weekend, but that I hadn't won either game. I couldn't believe my ears. After having my two best games in a Husky uniform, and doing everything humanly possible to win, he was putting the blame for the losses squarely on my shoulders. I got the feeling when I was talking to Greg, that he wasn't getting it. He was living in some parallel universe where not all is what it seems to be. I was being judged on my resume again, and I felt that I was in a no-win position, so I wasn't going to press the matter. He told me not to worry, that I would get to play a lot the rest of the season. I didn't really believe him, but there was nothing I could do. The only thing I could do was play, and play well.

As the season rolled along, I kept playing well when I was called upon. My previous year long slump was finally in the rearview mirror. Denny was still playing most of the games, but I was playing a fair bit. We had the UBC Alumni come to town. Denny played the Friday night game, as usual, and I was given the Saturday game. The Friday game was an easy win for us, but Saturday the Alumni cranked it up a bit. The game was tied 2-2 in the third period. One of the Alumni got the puck in the corner, and our defenseman had fallen down so that the Alumni guy had a clear track to the net. He skated until he was almost in front of the net and was pulling the puck to his backhand. I just kind of reached out and poked the puck away. Our defenseman, who had fallen in the corner, was now back in the play and took the puck. He passed it up to a forward, and they were gone. Meanwhile, the

UBC guy, who I had poked the puck away from, was standing there beside me. I looked at him, and he looked at me and he sighed, and said sadly, "I used to be SO fucking good." And then he skated away. The third period ended with the score 2-2. Five minutes of overtime, sudden death. The play went back and forth but neither team really had any good scoring chances. In the last 30 seconds, I was mentally preparing myself for the inevitable shootout, when Blair Brieman scored with 2 seconds left in OT. We win.

Because of Denny's work schedule, he wasn't quite as sharp as the previous season, and I had picked my play up quite a bit. I felt as the season rolled on that my position was getting more secure, and that I had finally earned the respect of my teammates, if not the coaches. We had a road trip to Anchorage that Denny couldn't go to. And instead of flying, we took the bus. Eight hours later, our bus ride to Anchorage is finally over. The trip there was fine, no problems. But we didn't bring a backup goalie. Nobody had said anything to me. I just assumed that none were available, and that I would be playing both games. We checked into our hotel and then got to the rink. Guess who walks in with his goalie equipment? Ken Kinney, my old high school friend. They had flown him in just for these games. I was glad to see him, but I wished someone would've told me that he was coming. Kenny and I got caught up with each other, and he told me about his wife and daughters and his career as a firefighter in Burnaby. He played the Friday game. He played well, but we lost. I played the Saturday game. I played solidly, but didn't make any big saves, and we lost. We left Anchorage right after the game, and on the drive back to Whitehorse, everybody was asleep. It was about 3 a.m., and I am about half way back in an aisle seat. I couldn't sleep. All of a sudden, the bus driver slams on the brakes hard, the bus comes lurching to a stop. I got up and headed to the front to see what was wrong. The bus driver was just sitting there staring out the window. When I got up to the front of the bus, I could see the problem. There were two Buffalos walking across the road. They were maybe four feet from the front of the bus and just coming into the glare of the headlights. They were huge and looked like mammoths. I couldn't believe the size of them. I wished to God that I had brought a camera. Nobody had one. It would have been nice to get a picture of them. They just ambled across the road, like a couple out for a Sunday stroll. Beautiful. It is one of my favourite memories of my time in the north. We arrived back in Whitehorse a few hours later. I went home to bed.

About Christmas time, it became apparent that Whitehorse was not going to be able to host the Allan Cup. The money just wasn't there. The tournament instead would be played in Quesnel. The Quesnel Millionaires, The Huskies, The Warroad Lakers, (from Minnesota, where they made Christian hockey sticks), and The Stony Plain Eagles would vie for the championship. I know behind the scenes everybody was working feverishly to get our team ready for the tournament.

Denny was always an aggressive goalie, and he would take his fair share of penalties. He would always give me a hard time, because during my entire tenure in Whitehorse, I had never been called for an infraction. Nobody had pissed me off enough, I guess. On our final trip to Fairbanks in 1993, Denny challenged me to get a penalty. I always had long hair during my senior hockey days. The guys all called it a mullet, but I preferred the term 'moulet'. After Christmas I had decided to chop it all off. I told the stylist to cut it all, except for a tail. One small inch wide strand of hair that would hang down past my shoulders. The guys hated it. They were always trying to cut it off. At parties I would have to stand with my back in a corner so no one could get behind me with any kind of cutting implement. Terrie hated it too. I was surprised that she never cut it off while I was asleep. So, we get to Fairbanks, Denny plays the Friday game, and I play the Saturday game. If I don't get a penalty, Denny gets to cut off my tail. By this time, I have played against Fairbanks so many times that the Gold Kings know me pretty well and know I'm not a dirty goalie by any stretch of the imagination. The puck drops and I'm not even concerning myself with stopping the puck. I'm determined to get a penalty. I figured it couldn't be that hard. I am hacking and whacking and punching guys, and the Gold Kings are all looking at me like I'm from Mars. The referee wouldn't even look in my direction. In the first period alone, I deserved at least six penalties, and he missed them all. The second period starts and same thing. I wasn't getting anywhere so figured I would try to get a Delay of Game penalty by shooting the puck over the glass. Late in the second period, I got a golden opportunity. The puck comes to me with no opposing player close by. I shoot the puck as high and as hard as I can, (Lance would have been proud of me. By now I could actually shoot the puck quite well left-handed), but the glass in their arena is quite high. The puck hit about six inches below the top of the glass and ricocheted to one of our players who went down and scored a goal. Great, I wanted a penalty, but I get an assist instead. I go back to hacking and slashing guys in front of the net. The referee is now noticing, but all he would do is wag his finger at me and say, "Calm down goalie." The third period starts, and I am now reaching desperation mode. No way I am losing my tail. I would've thrown my stick at the puck, but that would've been a penalty shot, and the game was close. I didn't want to risk losing the game just to get a penalty. An idea popped into my head, and I smiled like the Grinch when he came up with his plan to steal Christmas. With about 3 minutes left in the game, Denny calls me from the Bench, "Hey Jerry" (the "Teabag" nickname never really took hold in Whitehorse, even though everyone knew about it). I looked over and Lynn had given him a pair of scissors. He had them above his head and was doing the cutting motion. The final buzzer went, and we lost, but I don't remember the score. I went straight to the referee and said, "You suck, dickface!" and he puts his hands to his hips and says, "You got a misconduct!" Finally, I got my penalty. Denny comes racing up to me with the scissors, "Turn around, I get to cut off your tail!" I said, "Not a chance loser, I just got a misconduct." Denny's chin dropped to the ice, and he made a mad dash to the referee to find out if this was true. He came back laughing his head off, "You asshole! I can't believe you did that." We had a good laugh about it, and I kept my tail. I eventually got tired of standing in corners at parties and cut it off myself.

At Beaver Lumber, they were finishing construction on a new and larger store. It was completed close to the end of the hockey season. It was more than twice the size of the old one. With the building completed, all the inventory that hadn't been sold, needed to be moved. And all the new inventory had to be logged in and priced and tagged. It was a huge logistical undertaking. I had to work 12-hour days and Saturdays too. The regular season was over, but the team was still practicing for the Allan Cup. I wasn't able to make it most days. When things settled down at work, I went back to practice. Everybody knew that the team was still adding players, but exactly who, wasn't being shared. Ron and Greg kept that information close to the vest. For me, the big red flag was when we had a car wash to raise money for the trip to Quesnel. All the wives and girlfriends, and some of the players were there. The players were expected to wear their jerseys to attract fans of the team. When I got my familiar

#33, I unfolded it and my Hack name bar had been removed and replaced with Kinney. "Fuck this," I thought. Let Kinney get his own number. I knew I was going as the third goalie, but I liked my number and wanted to keep it. I would take it up later with the brass. I put tape over Kinney's name and washed cars all day.

Bobby House, who was a local from Whitehorse, was playing in the Western Hockey League. He had finished his season with the Brandon Wheat Kings and was coming to practice with us. He was a really nice kid. He was drafted by Chicago in the 3rd round and was looking like he might make the show in a couple of years. After practice one night, I challenged him. He lined up 10 pucks about 20 feet from the net. And I said, "Ok Bobby, show me what you got." He fired all 10 in about 10 seconds. He didn't hit me once, and he never missed the net. I think he hit the post once. Nobody told me at the time, but Bobby had the hardest slap shot in the Western Hockey League that year. Bobby never did make it to the NHL. He had a long career in the minors and then a few years in Europe before retiring in 2005.

I had worked enough overtime that my bosses said I could have the week off for the Allan Cup. We were due to leave at the end of the week. Two nights before our flight left, I was in Bill Hunter's Sporting Goods shop. Bill was on the executive, and I was just getting some last-minute things that I needed for the trip. I double checked with him about what time to be at the airport. Bill kind of grimaced, and I know it pained him to tell me, he said, "Jerry. I don't think you're going." I was stunned beyond belief. "What?" "Why?" He said that he didn't know that I didn't know. He told me to call Greg Anderson and get the story. I called Greg, and he told me there was only enough money to bring one goalie from Whitehorse, and that was Denny. He also said, "Let me make some calls and see if we can get you on that flight." I seriously doubted that he could. The night before the flight left, there was one more optional practice. Only about half the guys made it. After practice was over, Greg repeated that there was only enough money for one goalie to come from Whitehorse. Ken Kinney was coming up from Vancouver. I was crushed. Right down to my soul. Absolutely crushed. I felt like I had flown a little too close to the sun and got burned. Randy Merckel, one of our players came into the room and saw me sitting there by myself with my head in my hands. He asked me what was wrong. I told him that Greg had just told me that I wasn't going to Quesnel. Randy was pissed, but you could tell he was still excited to go. He felt bad for me. I told him not to worry about me, just go and win the fucking thing. He left. I'll always be grateful to Bill Hunter for having the courage to give me the bad news. If Bill hadn't told me I wasn't going, I would've shown up at the airport and would've suffered a level of humiliation so excruciating that it would've been hard to recover from. To this day, I don't understand how somebody, anybody, who was associated with the team, didn't think to tell me that I wasn't going to the Allan Cup. I'm just so glad that I went to Bill's shop that night.

The Native Tournament coincided with the Allan Cup that year, so I joined my friends The Nannock Warriors. One of the other teams had paid Tiger Williams a rumoured $10,000 to play in the tournament. When we played against him, my goal was to keep him off the scoresheet. He must've been in phenomenal shape, because I only saw him go to the bench once. Other than that, he played the entire game. He had a really heavy shot. He got me twice in the same spot on my thigh. I had a huge bruise for a week. I managed to keep him from scoring until the third period when he drilled a snapshot over my shoulder. It hit the crossbar, and then went in. I guess you don't score 241 goals in the NHL without any talent. We won the game, and we all got to meet Tiger afterwards. The Warriors went all the way to the final and won. I won best goalie and received a new blocker. What I needed was a new set of goalie pants, so I went to Bill's and traded the blocker in. He felt sorry for me and gave me a great deal. Winning the tournament was nice. The Warriors gave me $50 from the prize money, which was more than generous. Also, they said that since I had played two years in a row that I was an official member of the team, and they gave me this absolutely stunning light red and white leather team jacket with an embroidered team logo on the back. It must've been worth five or six hundred dollars. It took my breath away. It was nice to be appreciated, especially after what I had just gone through. I kept the jacket and held onto it for years. I kept it in a closet upstairs at my parent's house, but somebody must've seen it and liked it because one day it disappeared. Later that night, after the tournament was over, I heard that Whitehorse had won the Allan Cup. Fuck. I wanted to be happy for them, but I couldn't. I wanted to be happy for Denny and for Kenny. Kenny had been to the Allan Cup final once before with Abbotsford in 1990, but had lost to Montreal in 6 games. I was at a loss. I wanted to be happy for them, but I was just bitter beyond belief. I hated that feeling, it felt like I was contaminated with something.

Terrie had flown home to see her family and was coming back on the same flight as the team. I had to pick her up at the airport, but I wanted no part of any celebration. I stood far away from the arrivals gate. Terrie came off the plane just before the players. There was a small contingent of fans awaiting them. I saw Terrie and waved her over. She was about halfway to where I was standing when the players emerged. I just caught a glimpse of Greg Anderson carrying the trophy in, and the fans cheering. I wanted to puke. Terrie got to me and was a little bit puzzled. We hadn't talked the entire time she was gone. I gave her a brief rundown of what had transpired. Then I told her, "First, they leave me behind, then they have to go and win the fucking thing." I told her how pissed off I was, and that I hated Greg and Ron, and that we were leaving town as soon as possible. I wanted to go home.

After the Allan Cup, there were a couple of celebrations in town. I didn't attend. After a couple of weeks, I hadn't heard from anybody connected to the team, except for Denny. And Randy Merckel had made it a point to come in to Beaver Lumber to see me. He said that he thought at times this year I was playing better than Denny and that it was bullshit that I got left behind. I told him that I appreciated it, but I didn't really want to talk about it. I congratulated him and said I was happy for him. It was a great accomplishment. The rumour around town was that the team was folding. I wasn't surprised.

I found out later that the Huskies had a 3rd goalie with them. His name was Lance Carlson, and they had flown him up with Ken Kinney. He had played some junior hockey with New Westminster and Portland, and a little bit of pro in the East Coast league, (with Rob Hrytsak no less). Someone also told me that he was injured and couldn't have played if they needed him to. This made me even more bitter. An injured goalie who had played junior was a better choice than me? Oh, my fucking God. If Greg Anderson had been standing there when I had found that out, I would've ripped him a new asshole. When I spoke with Denny and told him that I was happy for him, but that I was really bitter about being left behind. Denny told me that it might've been a little more than I could handle. That the team from Warroad should've won, that they were a powerhouse team and that the Huskies got lucky when Quesnel took them out. I told Denny that I had played that Warroad team when I was in Assiniboia, and had beaten them twice. In the end it didn't matter though. What's done is done, and I was moving on. The raw bitterness would eventually fade, but it still affects me to this day. It struck at my core. I find that I don't trust quite as easy, and I'm a little more cynical when it comes to people who are in a position of even the slightest power. Denny and I would remain friends for quite a few years. Then we lost track of each other, and I haven't heard from him for awhile. I hope he's doing well. He's still the best goalie I ever played with or against. Just a side note, the Warroad Lakers won the next three Allan Cups.

Terrie and I gave our two weeks-notice at work, and the day before our last day, I pulled Don Corothers aside and thanked him for the job and everything else he had done for me. On top of being a world class businessman, he was also an extremely decent human being. He was one of those people who have a gruff exterior, but underneath is a heart of gold. I told him that I was only 31 and I still wanted to play hockey, and that the Huskies were folding, so I had to go elsewhere. I was hoping that Darryl Lauer was looking for a goalie in Fresno. Maybe I could finish what I started in California. On my last day of work, I was just walking out of the building when I ran into Greg Anderson in the parking lot. He was all friendly and effusive, like we were buddies. I wanted to slap him, but I just played along. After our brief conversation had ended, I walked away and muttered under my breath, "peckerhead jerkenstein." Looking back on it now, I have to give Greg and Ron the benefit of the doubt. I don't know that it was they who made the decision to leave me behind. It may have been made higher up, and their hands were tied. Some things you just never know.

The only player on the Huskies that I was truly happy for was Darryl Sturko. He was one of my good friends on the team. This was the story I was told, and I can't say if it's true or not, but I hope it is. Sometime after the team had won the Allan Cup, Sturko and his family planned a trip to Toronto to see the Hockey Hall of Fame. Unknown to Darryl, the Hall of Fame recognizes every Allan Cup winning team by taking one jersey from that team and placing it in a display case. And for the Huskies, they chose Sturko's jersey. I can't imagine what it was like for Sturko to walk into the Hall of Fame and see his jersey hanging there. Kudos to you Sturks, you deserve it. I hope your jersey is there when I finally get to see the H.O.F.

As soon as we could, Terrie and I made a mad dash for Vancouver. I phoned ahead and got my job back installing paving stones. That would take care of the summer. Terrie wanted to be closer to her family, so she was going to go to Calgary and if I couldn't go to California, I would join her there.

A couple of weeks after we got home, I gave Darryl Lauer a call. He remembered me and actually sounded excited about the prospect of me coming to Fresno again. He said he would be in touch. Darryl phoned me a few weeks later and informed me that he was no longer coach and GM of the Fresno Falcons. They had relieved him of his duties and if I wanted to, I could give the new guy a call. His name was John Olver. I gave the man a call. I told him my story, and he said, "Uh-huh." He said that he had never heard of me. Well, colour me shocked. He said that he wanted only Americans on the team, or imports that were legally entitled to work there. And that the only goalies he'd be interested in were guys like Ken Kinney or Lance Carlson. Great, those names again. I wanted to jump through the phone and slap the guy. My senior hockey career had just come to a sudden and ignominious end with a big loud thud. And I'm reminded one more time that I'm still a hockey nobody. If you're wondering why I didn't just go back to Assiniboia, the Southern Rebels senior team had folded, and they began a very successful junior B program that still runs today.

Terrie and I parted ways. As wonderful as she was and as much as I loved her, she was a country girl, and I was a city boy. She couldn't live in Vancouver, and I couldn't live anywhere else, not permanently anyway. We could never really bridge that gap. But we shared a lot of really great times over the five years we were together. I will always remember her great sense of humour. She forever has a piece of my heart. She got married to a really good guy and they have a son and daughter. Dawson and Landry. Dawson is a football player. I told Terrie that I find it disturbing that he is not a goalie. She thinks I'm an idiot. We remain good friends to this day.

Knowing that my Senior hockey career was over, I decided to take a year off and live on my unemployment benefits. I started to look for a team to play for. In the Province newspaper, in the same sports section that I first saw the ad that a hockey team in Saskatchewan was looking for players, they had this thing called, "The Noticeboard." If anybody wanted to buy or sell something sports related, or if they were advertising for a fundraiser, or looking for players, they would put an ad in The Noticeboard. I saw an ad that a team was looking for a goalie for the upcoming season in the VAHA. I thought this would be perfect. They wouldn't be looking for someone with junior or pro experience, and, for once, they should be extremely impressed with my resume. Finally, I would be dealing from a position of strength. I phoned the number and talked to a guy named Clint. I told him that I had just finished playing five and a half years of "semi-pro", (most people, if you tell them you played senior hockey, they think you mean Oldtimers), and that I had a deal to go to California to play, but that it had fallen through, and now I was looking for a team to play for. Clint said, "Uh-huh."

"Oh God," I thought, "Does this never end?"

Epilogue

Clint, the man I spoke to on the phone, was Clint Farrell. He ran a team called the Lansdowne Knights who played in the VAHA. He said his reaction was due to the many responses he had gotten from the Noticeboard ad. A lot of guys had given him a story similar to mine, and when push came to shove, they just weren't very good. I ended up playing for Lansdowne for the next 18 years until they folded in 2011.

I played two more seasons of senior hockey, starting at the age of 40, with a team called the New Westminster Beavers, who ironically, played in Abbotsford. My family was finally able to come out and watch me play for the first time. In my first year with the Beavers, we won the Coy Cup, symbolic of British Columbia's Senior A Championship. But lost to Campbell River in the playdowns the next season. The team folded after that. It's kind of weird that teams seem to fold after I played for them.

Just one final note about my senior hockey career. I've never been a big believer in statistics. I like the quote from Bobby Bragan, who was a baseball player in the early 20th century. I'm paraphrasing but I believe he said, "The problem with statistics is, if you have one foot on fire and the other in a bucket of ice, according to the statisticians, you should be perfectly comfortable". In the 4 seasons that I played for the Rebels, I won the Best Goalie trophy every year. 11 other goalies came and went during that time, some specifically to take my spot. I also won the league trophy for Best Goals Against Average every year. In 35 years of playing competitive hockey, I won a lot of trophies. The danger of winning that many is that you can start to think that you're better than you are, (I call it "The Red Light Lonnie Syndrome"). I only kept one trophy from all those years and my wife is under strict instructions to show it to me if my head starts to get too big. I assumed that when the league bought the trophy that year, they sent it out to be engraved in a shop that didn't employ sports fans. When I won the Best Goals Against award and it was presented to me, I read the inscription and it read:

"Best Average Goalie"
"Jerry Hack"

How apt is that?

The last team I played for is called Harlem, (long story). I played with them from 2005 until my retirement from playing at the age of 52, in 2014. I had always told people jokingly that as long as Chris Chelios was playing, my dream was alive. He finally retired in 2010 and the dream was dust. My last game of ice hockey was played against a team called The Bucks in the regional playdowns in what is now the Canlan 8 Rinks league (The 4 Rinks expanded to 8 in 1995). We lost 2-1 but I had my best game of the year, and it was a good way to go out. To finish my career with this team, and these guys, was the perfect ending. Everybody on the team, and their families, all hang out and get along like one big happy family, and the team is filled with a bunch of characters (I could write a book). At the end of my final season, Harlem did me the honour of retiring my jersey. They might have done it just to make sure that I wouldn't come back, but I'm hoping that's not the case. They surprised me with it at a team party. The jersey hangs in my house in a beautiful frame. A big thank you to Tone, Mixey, T-Dub, Salty, Brock, Cujo, Eddie, O-Town, Bladesy, Arnie, Lomax, Nate Dogg, and Dario. My Harlem brothers forever.

After my playing career ended, I tried my hand at refereeing beer league hockey. It was more fun than I'd thought it would be. But in the summer of 2018, I was diagnosed with a severe case of Rheumatoid Arthritis. Since I am unable to tie my skates, I am now just a spectator, which is ok with me. I'm fine with it. People still ask me what I think would've happened if I had started playing ice hockey when I was a kid. That maybe I would've made it all the way to "The Show". I assure them that I most likely would've ended up in the exact same place. I tell them that I pretty much maxed out any potential I ever had, and I was glad that I had taken the shot. I didn't make it very far, but I made it farther than 95% of all my fellow schmucks who ever laced on a pair of skates. I can honestly say that I lived my dream, I got paid to play hockey, and I would not trade that for anything. Sure, there was some heartbreak, but it was mostly good, a little bit great, and a whole lot of fun while it lasted. I can't tell you how many times in the past when I would be working away and a memory of my hockey days would pop into my head, and I couldn't help but smile and laugh. People would look at me strange because I'd be somewhere with no one around me, laughing my head off.

Tye Fitzsimmons passed away in 2016. I'm hoping that he and Randy are playing hockey together again. It's a big reason why I wrote this book. I know so little about my parent's upbringing, and they are gone now, so I can't ask them, and I didn't want to leave this life without my daughter Brooklynn knowing my story, or at least a good part of it. You are missed Tye. Thank you for being such a great guy, you will never be forgotten. R.I.P. my friend.

Grant Sandbeck and Kevin Tendler also passed away recently and have memorial pages on Facebook. I will never forget the great times we shared together, and my heart goes out to their families.

John Aitken and I lost touch after his mom passed away in 1999. We recently reconnected while I was researching this book. He lives on Vancouver Island and is doing ok. He's close to 70 years old now and has some health issues but remains the same great guy he always was. His sister Cheryl passed away in 2005, the same year my sister Marlene left us.

I work at a job now that I have had for the last 25 years. I like the people I work with. I am married to a beautiful woman, and have a 12-year old daughter who is the light of my life. She has me tied around her little finger, (I like it there). Life is good. My cup runneth over. And, if I'm allowed to quote Steve Martin from "The Jerk" one last time, "I know the difference between Shit and Shinola."

What a long strange trip it's been, and it ain't quite over yet.

That's my story and I'm sticking to it.

Teabag

Just for shits and giggles here is a list of all the teams that I can remember playing for. I am sure I am missing some.

Burnaby Kings
Burnaby Golden Bears
Cottrell Forwarding Buzzards
Freightliner Eagles
Instabox Jets
Ibox Flabby Cats
Admirals
Lansdowne Knights
Assiniboia Southern Rebels
Whitehorse Huskies
Pineriders
Broncos
Chiefs
Hanson Bros.
Pacific Chiefs
Pats
Helijet
Fridge Guys
Selects
ACT Selects
Bandits
Cobras
Pit Stop Posse
Burnaby Blues
Bombers
Hornets

Cowboys
Hound Dogs
Ice Agers
Burnaby Warriors
Bingers
Hub International Panthers
Bad Xample
Labatt Blues
Regina Blues
Shark Club
Unity Telecom Eagles
Burnaby Rangers
Dog River Ratdogs
Satan
Blunt Bros.
Beaver Lumber
New Westminster Beavers
Nannock Warriors
Harlem
Vikings
Alers
Evil Beaver
Tribe
Tallboys
Knights
Squamish Eagles

Made in United States
North Haven, CT
30 December 2022

30370679R00138